A
Just Peace
Church

A Just Peace Church

THE PEACE THEOLOGY DEVELOPMENT TEAM

Edited by Susan Thistlethwaite

Produced by
The Office for Church in Society
United Church of Christ

United Church Press
New York

The biblical quotations have been adapted from the *Revised Standard Version
of the Bible*, copyright 1946, 1952, and © 1971, 1973 by the Division of
Christian Education, National Council of Churches, and are used with
permission.

Library of Congress Cataloging-in-Publication Data

A Just peace church.

    1. Peace—Religious aspects—Christianity. 2. United Church of Christ—
Doctrines. 3. United Churches—Doctrines. I. Thistlethwaite, Susan Brooks,
1948-   . II. Peace Theology Development Team. III. United Church of
Christ. Office for Church in Society.
BT 736.4.J87 1986   261.8'73   86-11276
ISBN 0-8298-0587-7 (pbk.)

United Church Press, 132 West 31 Street, New York, NY 10001

Although the doctrine of the "just war" is a
venerable one in the church, it is becoming
increasingly clear that the classical criteria which
the theologians have used to classify wars as "just"
or "unjust" will no longer serve. *In our kind of
world, war has become dysfunctional.* We now need
to put as much effort into defining a just peace as
we have done in the past in defining a just war.
    Robert V. Moss
            United Church Herald supplement, 1971

This book is dedicated
to the memory of Dr. Robert V. Moss,
second president of the United Church of Christ

CONTENTS

PREFACE

"COURAGE IN THE struggle for justice and peace" is one of the powerful affirmations in the United Church of Christ Statement of Faith. It is central to the identity of our church. It is one of our most ardent prayers and richest blessings. To be part of the United Church of Christ is to be part of the struggle for justice and peace.

In June of 1985 the Fifteenth General Synod, meeting in Ames, Iowa, took two important actions to strengthen this identity. They declared justice and peace to be two of the priorities of the church for the next four years. And they passed a Pronouncement "Affirming the United Church of Christ to be a Just Peace Church."

This Pronouncement, and the accompanying Proposal for Action (chapter 8 of this book), were produced after four years of work by a Peace Theology Development Team as it sought to discover and develop the theological roots of the peacemaking identity of the United Church of Christ.

This process began in 1981 when the Thirteenth General Synod, appealing to "the traditional stand of the UCC [which] has called for its members to be peacemakers and to work diligently for justice, human rights, and peace within the family of nations," voted to "become a peace church." The resolution had been brought to General Synod by Roger McDougle, a youth delegate from the Kansas-Oklahoma Conference. The original wording of the resolution called upon the United Church of Christ to *declare* itself a *pacifist* church. The Synod amended the resolution, calling instead for the United Church to *become* a *peace* church.

The word pacifist was a source of concern to the Thirteenth General Synod. Two years later, at the Fourteenth General Synod, even the words peace church were a source of concern, and a resolution on the floor was amended to read "peacemaking church." Both Synods were signaling that peace is central to the identity of the United Church of Christ. Both also seemed unclear about what peace means and what it means for the United Church of Christ to become more intentional in this identity.

Although the Thirteenth General Synod called for the United Church of Christ to "become a peace church," it did not spell out how this might happen. The UCC Office for Church in Society appointed a Peace Theology Development Team to begin reflecting on the meaning of peace and its centrality to our identity. Two years later this team was commissioned by the Fourteenth General Synod to consider more fully the bases and ramifications—theologically, politically, programmatically—of becoming a peacemaking church.

The Peace Theology Development Team offers this document as a beginning theological statement on peace specifically for the United Church of Christ.

The team members are as follows:

Sue Garman, member and former chair of the Peace Among the Nations Committee; former staff member of the South Central Conference, UCC, Houston, Texas

Elly Haney, peace coordinator, Maine Conference, UCC; coordinator, Feminist Spiritual Community of Portland, Maine

Cynthia Ikuta, chair of the team, UCC pastor serving First Baptist Church of Enfield Center, New York; member, Commission for Racial Justice, UCC

Robert Jones, co-pastor, College Hill Community
    Church, Dayton, Ohio; adjunct faculty and director,
    Center for Urban Studies Metropolitan Ministry,
    United Theological Seminary, Dayton
Mineo Katagiri, conference minister (retired), Northern
    California Conference
Charles Kriete, chaplain, USAC (retired); former
    instructor, Army Way College, Carlisle,
    Pennsylvania (resigned from team, summer 1984)
Robert Lee, senior minister, First Congregational
    Church, Wilmette, Illinois
Jay Lintner, staff member to the team; peace priority
    coordinator and now director of the Washington
    Office, Office for Church in Society, UCC,
    Washington, DC.
Douglas Meeks, professor of systematic theology and
    philosophy, Eden Theological Seminary, St. Louis,
    Missouri
Olgha Sandman, director of Illinois Farm Worker
    Ministry; member of the Executive Committee,
    Council for Hispanic Ministries
Susan Thistlethwaite, assistant professor, theology and
    culture, Chicago Theological Seminary; editor of *A
    Just Peace Church*
Frederick Trost, conference minister, Wisconsin
    Conference, UCC.

The team met, discussed, and struggled together for
two to three days every three to six months over the
past three years. Various members wrote sections of the
document, which were critiqued by the whole team
and edited by Susan Thistlethwaite with help from Sue
Garman and Jay Lintner. The Pronouncement and
Proposal for Action, chapter 8, were drafted by Jay
Lintner; they were debated and amended by the
Directorate for the Office for Church in Society and then

by General Synod XV meeting in Ames, Iowa, June 1985.

The first draft of this document was published in October 1984 and circulated widely throughout the church. Many people and groups reacted to this draft, sending in hundreds of pages in response. The first draft and the response to it became the basis for the Pronouncement and the Proposal for Action, which were sent to the Fifteenth General Synod. The debate and the action of that synod have, in turn, provided a basis for the redrafting of this final version of *A Just Peace Church*.

What has been accomplished by this process and what does this book attempt to do? Several giant steps forward have been taken in this book and in the United Church of Christ declaring itself to be a Just Peace church:

- It affirms that making peace and doing justice are the task of Christians given to them by God in the shalom vision.
- It attempts to develop a new theological language or theological paradigm of peace theology, moving beyond the historic three peace paradigms: pacifism, just war, and crusade.
- It places the United Church of Christ in opposition to the institution of war.
- It places the United Church of Christ in opposition to the doctrine of nuclear deterrence, joining the larger church in the process of withdrawing moral sanction from this doctrine and insisting that new doctrines of common security be developed.
- It defines a Just Peace as shalom, the interrelation of friendship, justice, and common security from violence, underlining the linkage between peace and justice with the phrase "a Just Peace," and insisting that the search for disarmament and conflict

resolution must be accompanied by the search for justice.

- It affirms that all humans have a right to their basic human needs, including food, health care, housing, employment, and education.
- It affirms that the struggle for a Just Peace must be seen from and must learn from the perspective of the poor who are in the struggle for liberation.
- It stresses the critical historical moment in which we live and calls upon the church to recognize God's calling to an essential role in this moment.

We offer this book to the church in the hope that it will help in the process of planetary transformation.

Yvonne Delk, Executive Director

Jay Lintner, Staff to the Peace Theology Development Team

Office for Church in Society
United Church of Christ

1. INTRODUCTION

THE CHURCH IS the Body of the Risen Christ, the human vessel through and in which the Spirit of the Holy One continues the work of reconciliation and atonement made manifest in the life, death, and resurrection of Jesus of Nazareth. It is a human vessel, fraught with all the frailties and limitations inherent in every mortal being. It is not the Christ, but it exists to bear witness to the Christ and to the realm of God, which our Sovereign declared to be at hand.

"For just as the body is one and has many members," the apostle Paul said, "and all the members of the body, though many, are one body, so it is with Christ [1 Cor. 12:12]." He went on to say, "Now you are the body of Christ and individually members of it [1 Cor. 12:27]." This image continues to describe the Body of Christ in our time. We remain many parts—individuals, local congregations, associations, conferences, instrumentalities, synods, and denominations. Paul reminds us that the body is not to be identified with any one of its parts.

A signal mark of the Body of the Risen Christ throughout history has been Christ's prayer, expressed in word and deed, "Your realm come, your will be done, on earth as it is in heaven." In so saying we acknowledge and bear witness to the truth that the Creating-Redeeming-Sustaining God has a divine purpose and will for creation. It is not yet here, but it will come. As members of this Body, we "desire a better country, that is, a heavenly one," and thus are compelled to consider ourselves as "strangers and exiles on the earth [Heb. 11:13, 16]."

In so saying, however, we do not imply that we as Christian men and women can or should consider ourselves as being unrelated to or uninvolved in the affairs of this earth. "I do not pray," Jesus said on the night of his arrest, "that you should take them out of the world, . . . even as I am not of the world. Sanctify them in the truth; your word is truth. As you sent me into the world, so I have sent them into the world [John 17:15–18]." To the disciples, moreover, our Sovereign said: "You are the salt of the earth. . . . You are the light of the world [Matt. 5:13, 14]." Both images are compelling ones for Christians in this age. Salt in the first century A.D. was a life-sustaining preservative. Light, then as now, is that which enables people to see clearly what lies before them.

It is the calling of the church, in every age and place, to bear witness by word and deed to the realm of God, which is the Holy One's divine will for creation. As parts of that Body, we do this humbly and boldly— boldly because it is God's realm we bear witness to, not our own; humbly because we are but a part of the whole Body and thus "see as in a mirror darkly." We do not have, in other words, a warrant to usher in God's realm forcibly; we do have a mandate to bear witness by our whole lives to the vision of God's realm, which the Spirit has enabled us to perceive.

A Just Peace is our understanding of God's will for humankind. The definition of a "Just Peace" is based on the concept of peace expressed by the Hebrew word *shalom* as it is used biblically. The Old Testament scholar Gerhard von Rad defines "shalom" not as some inner, personal, pietistic possession, but as a communal well-being in which God's creation is justly ordered. It is a state of existence in which all aspects of God's creation play their individual roles harmoniously for the good of the whole.

Often, the peace to which most people refer when they use the word peace is symptomatic of the absence of the real peace, a Just Peace, which Jesus referred to when he approached the great city of Jerusalem. There on the hillside as he looked down on the city, seeing its injustices, the hunger, corruption, violence, and the vying for power, he wept and said: "If only today you knew the things that make for peace." Peace is not merely the absence of war but the presence of just social relations.

Historically and recently, segments of the church in the United States and worldwide have taken an active part in the movement for peace. In May 1983, for example, the Catholic Bishops' Conference wrote a pastoral letter on peace, which opened with a statement about the "new moment in history" to which the nuclear arms race has brought us, a moment that confronts the superpowers with the choice between reconciliation and mutual annihilation. But participation in the movement for peace has grown far beyond the circle of people led by conscience and faith. People normally lukewarm to social issues have also suddenly become aware of the "new moment in history" and its inherent threat to their lives, the lives of their children, and perhaps the whole earth. In many quarters, religious and secular, people have begun to discern this decisive historical moment. Doctors, scientists, teachers, students, and parents, churched and unchurched, have all joined the outpouring of energy to turn the arms race around.

For many church people, the burgeoning growth in military technology and the quantity of weapons means that peacemaking efforts are not only "political" and/or "prophetic" but *pastoral*. For church people, the passion for stopping the arms race is ignited by their commitment to the gospel, their understanding of faith, the love of their children, and the pain of seeing their children caught in the fear of nuclear war.

But the new passion for disarmament has encountered the ongoing commitment of the church to justice. Although black leaders from Martin Luther King Jr. and Andrew Young to Jesse Jackson have critized the arms race, the movement for disarmament has been less successful in capturing the heart, mind, and will of racial minorities committed to bringing justice to the world. This community has reminded the larger community that preoccupation with nuclear war has diverted attention from issues such as health, hunger, housing, and employment. They have been concerned—and often rightly so—that many of the new converts to the "peace movement" have been motivated more by the fear of losing their accustomed comforts than by the genuine desire to transform the inequities of the social and economic system of which the arms race is both a symptom and a driving force.

In the midst of all the concern, what might it mean for the United Church of Christ to "become a peace church"? The term "peace church" immediately calls to mind the Friends (Quakers), Mennonites, and the Church of the Brethren, whose enduring witness for peace and reconciliation has much to teach us. Indeed the United Church joins them in yearning and working for a world free of weapons and warfare.

10

But the history and strengths of the UCC differ. These other groups have emphasized opposition to warfare and violence more strongly than we have so far in our history. Yet, the United Church has made some commitments in the area of justice and equity. Under our church's strong black leadership during the ferment of the 1960s, for example, our part in the struggle for civil rights led to the establishment of the Commission for Racial Justice and its defense of the Wilmington Ten. With that commission's help, racial caucuses (Council on American Indian Ministries and United Black Christians) were formed to address the needs and voice the perspectives of other peoples of color. Similarly, with the rise of the women's movement in the 1970s, the United Church of Christ established a task force which led to a Coordinating Center for Women, advocated equal rights and other women's issues, encouraged women in the ordained ministry, and sought more intentionally to include women in the language and imagery of worship, discussion, and study.

To those most eager for change, our church's commitment has often been too little and too late. But it is clear that new winds of the Spirit are moving through the whole church. The Word has begun to speak through people never heard from before. The English, Swiss, and German men who shaped the Reformation faith are being joined by women and African, Asian, Hispanic, and Native American men and women, who bring us different experiences and insights, languages, and cultures. These contemporary men and women wrote none of the creeds, treatises, or formulations of the past, so their story has not yet been claimed as part of the church's "tradition." Instead, their experiences of injustice and oppression have led them to tell a new story. This "new story" is really an old story—the story of a God who calls slaves into freedom and chooses a Savior to bring good news to the poor. These people bring new life to the biblical story because they recognize in it their own stories of suffering and liberation.

Thus, they, too, call us to discern a "new moment in history." For them, however, the "new moment" is emerging not from the threat of nuclear annihilation, but from a new-found sense of dignity and hope. The "new moment" in our own history and theology is sparked by contributions heretofore overlooked, ignored, and forgotten. In the Reformation it may have been the fathers who preached about justice and mercy, but these "new voices," speaking from the experience of oppression, bring a new urgency to that message. Speaking from the "under-side," these new voices call Christians today to interpret the scriptures and our faith from the vantage point of the poor, the marginated, the disenfranchised, the landless, and the powerless, those to whom God spoke so decisively through Moses, Jesus, and the prophets. Given social and economic structures that curse the few with riches and the many with poverty, Christians must choose sides: we must challenge those structures actively or support them passively. These new voices are radically re-forming our faith by calling us to stand consciously with the poor and the powerless and showing us that that is where God has chosen to stand. We now call everyone to use his or her special gifts, talents, and position in life to help move the current order toward one in which harmony and equity prevail.

This document begins (chapter 2) by outlining not only understandings of war and peace developed throughout the history of the church and the four denominational forebears of the United Church of Christ, but also those of the ethnic churches, and of women, which emerged with their traditions in the last century. This whole heritage is considered in light of the following factors: the context of conflict between the rich and poor within and among nations, the burgeoning arms race and continuing Cold War, and the increasing despair over whether the nuclear juggernaut can be controlled.

The new *historical* situation brings Christians to a new *theological* situation as well.

Chapter 3 presents "A Just Peace" as the starting point for interpreting our faith in this age. The Just Peace theology begins in the biblical definition of "shalom." Voices in the struggle for the shalom vision are the voice of God calling us to make peace with justice today. Chapter 4 presents the theological vision of shalom in order to ground the United Church of Christ as a church in a theology of peace with justice. In contrast to many religious documents produced on peace, this effort has the identity of the *church* and peace as its central focus.

In chapter 4, the doctrine of God is characterized by "friendship": a covenantal relationship of equality, security, unity, justice, and power. The unveiling of this aspect of our relationship with God helps us to understand the reign toward which God is pulling human history. This section also reflects on Jesus' revelations about power, freedom, and relationships with other people and God; and it reflects on the Holy Spirit, which nurtures us, sustains us, and strengthens us to resist the forces of evil. This section proposes a positive view of the state—that it may not only protect its people from violence by exerting force but also help create conditions of love and justice. Finally, it presents the theological grounding for our vision of alternative forms of society.

Chapter 5 elaborates this vision that the Just Peace church offers to the state. It has been entitled "Real Security."

Chapter 6 reports on and suggests ways to respond to the Just Peace vision. It suggests liturgical, sacramental, and educational means for engaging our church more fully in the quest for a Just Peace. Chapter 7 explores the question of what structure might better embody our commitment to be a Just Peace church.

Finally, chapter 8 contains the Pronouncement and Proposal for Action. Chapter 9 is a study guide.

In our concern for justice, we on the team have searched for language to express the vision of a world characterized by shared access to resources and power, a world free from violence, warfare, and greed. We want to make clear that by "peace" we meant both the pursuit of disarmament and the transformation of the social and economic relationships that at present inevitably lead to war. But, because for many people "peace" has acquired a limited meaning (such as opposition to a specific war or weapons system or work toward a "nuclear freeze"), the simple term "peace church" was problematic. We considered the term "peacemaking church" in order to emphasize the active creation of peace, but it, too, was problematic: "peacemaking" (as in "peacemaking" troops and missiles) is too often used in government and military jargon as doublespeak for war making; others use the term to mean "pacifying," without attention to the justice dimension of real peace. We have chosen the term "A Just Peace Church" to begin to identify the United Church of Christ, in an attempt to suggest some of the fullness of equity and harmony embodied in the biblical concept of shalom.

2.

THE CONTEXT FOR PEACE THEOLOGY IN THE UNITED CHURCH OF CHRIST

The Church's Historical Approaches to Peace, War, and Violence

HISTORICALLY, the Christian church at various times and among various groups has taken three approaches to questions of violence, war, and a Just Peace: pacifism, just war, and crusade.

PACIFISM

The first approach, pacifism, opposes the taking of any life and urges Christians not to serve in the military or participate in war. Generally, it opposes all acts of violence, even those that intend to prevent greater violence. This was the predominant view of the church during its first three centuries, before Christianity was legalized under Theodosius and institutionalized by Constantine.

In every century, some Christians have chosen to renounce violence altogether, often citing as their authority those sayings of Jesus that oppose resisting evil or returning evil for evil. Historically, however, pacifists have understood and practiced their beliefs in a variety of ways.

The early church tended to withdraw generally from worldly life. Christians were an outlawed minority because they would not swear an oath of loyalty to Caesar, who was regarded by other citizens as God. Hence the Christians' refusal to participate in war was closely related to their refusal to participate in idolatry.

In the Reformation era and after, Anabaptists and others put their emphasis on the role of suffering in Christian ethics. Continuing in this line, Mahatma Gandhi, Dorothy Day, and Martin Luther King Jr. have had profound impact in showing the ability of pacifists to transform social situations as part of an activist strategy for social change.

Some pacifists have held that pacifism means that under no circumstances should violence ever be used. Others, who approve of force being used to uphold the rule of law, emphasize pacifism as a method of unexpectedly transforming violent social situations by grace and surprising forgiveness.

While three main "peace," or pacifist, denominations exist today in the United States— Mennonites, Church of the Brethren, and Quakers— there have always been many pacifists in Catholic and mainline Protestant churches, including the United Church of Christ.

JUST WAR

During the sack of Rome in the fifth century, Augustine developed the second approach, the doctrine of just war, in recognition of the Christian's duty to preserve order and defend a neighbor. The doctrine was not intended to justify war but, rather, to limit it. It was meant to constrain both the reasons for which war could be initiated and to limit a war's destructiveness once it had begun.

The criteria for initiating war are as follows:

- Because war must serve the common good of society it must be declared by a legitimate authority. (On the basis of this criterion, both the Vietnam War and the Falkland Islands War were unjust wars.)
- War must be waged with good intention.
- War must lead to a good outcome; the situation after war must be more humane than the situation before it.
- War must be the last resort for conflict resolution; all peaceful means must have been exhausted.
- War must be waged for defensive and not offensive reasons. (Augustine did not include self-defense as a valid reason for taking another's life, but Aquinas added it eight centuries later.)

The criteria for limiting destruction are these:

- The means of war must be proportional to the ends; the methods must not be worse than the evil opposed.
- Combatants must be distinguished from citizens; the civil population must not be attacked. (This principle was violated by the Northern general W.T. Sherman in the American Civil War and by both sides in World War II.)

Both Augustine and Aquinas believed that *all* criteria must be met for war to be considered just.

The third approach, crusade, is the conviction that God sanctions war when the enemy represents great evil. This view found early expression in some of the Old Testament conquest narratives, especially those urging the total destruction of enemy persons and property. It was perhaps most fully articulated during the Middle Ages, when the nations of Western Christendom sought to win back the Holy Lands from Islam.

Although most modern ethicists, secular or religious, claim to adhere either to the pacifist or just-war theories, the crusade theory endures, however unacknowledged. From characterizations of the Soviet Union as an "evil empire" to the freedom fighter's conviction that "God is on our side" (and the U.S. justification for the bombing of cities "because Hitler must be stopped"), the crusade theory seems to persist with considerable force in modern rhetoric and practice.

Before examining other characteristics of the contemporary discussion of war and peace, however, it is necessary to define sharply the memory and identity of the United Church of Christ on these issues.

Our Denominational Heritage

The Free Church, Evangelical, and Reformed traditions that comprise our inheritance in the United Church of Christ provide no unequivocal conclusions for our times regarding questions of peace, war, and violence. Our history and theology differ widely from those of the historic "peace churces"; the Reformation traditions of Luther, Zwingli, and Calvin rejected the pacifism of the Anabaptists and embraced the

Augustinian just-war tradition. What in our tradition, then, calls us to identify ourselves as a Just Peace church?

In the teaching of Luther, Christians belong simultaneously to both the kingdom of God and the kingdom of the world. As members of God's kingdom, Christians live in love; never may they "wield the sword" on their own behalf. As members of the world, however, Christians have an active duty to bear arms to preserve order and protect their neighbors. Thus, in spite of his initial sympathy for the peasants' grievances, Luther condemned any violent effort to change the secular political order and finally virulently opposed their uprising. War must be waged only by the proper authorities and only as a last resort; it has to be defensive and motivated by a just cause. Luther's radical separation of the religious and secular led him to reject religious or pseudo-religious crusades. In his *War Against the Turk*, he held that Christians fight the Turks not as Christians but as citizens in defense of their territory.

Although he was not an absolute pacifist, the young Zwingli was a strong advocate of peace. He believed that Swiss participation in mercenary service led to needless bloodshed, the waste of young men's lives, and the corruption of human souls. Toward the end of his short career, as European politics rocked from the divisions of the Reformation, he encouraged the preaching of the gospel against the Catholic Hapsburgs to the north and the Catholic Swiss cantons to the south. Faced with Catholic military action, he urged the Protestant cantons of Zurich and Bern to defend their territories. He died in battle as a chaplain to the forces of Zurich.

Like Zwingli, Calvin strongly opposed militarism and the involvement of the Swiss in mercenary service.

He recognized that, more often than not, wars were senseless exhibitions of humanity's base nature. But, like Luther, he believed that war was sometimes necessary to punish evil in an imperfect world. In such situations, Calvin believed that recourse to warfare may be adopted, but war may be conducted only for a legitimate cause and for the defense of a state— provided that all other efforts at securing the peace have failed. Even in just wars, according to Calvin, damage to the people and the environment must be restrained as far as possible.

> God bridles the license to make damages in the midst of war ardor . . . though the law of war opens the door to plunder, pillage, and excess, yet as far as possible one ought to guard himself that the soil be not spoiled and disfigured to the point of being made barren for the future. In brief, when he ought not to lose view of the utilities of humankind.

The Huguenots in France in the sixteenth century and the Puritan supporters of Cromwell in the seventeenth century departed from these just-war advocates and preached a religious crusade. "To fight for God's glory on earth, for the advancement of the gospel, to avenge God upon the idolaters" were all urged in Puritan sermons as legitimate reasons for warfare.

The New England Puritans continued to interpret their cause as the cause of God. Fired by the fervor of the Great Awakening, these Puritan and Reformed churches, as well as some German Lutheran churches in Pennsylvania, made the patriot cause into a religious one. They meant not only to create an American union but to bring about the reign of God in the new land.

The first two wars fought by the new nation, however, attracted considerable opposition from New England Congregationalists, who together with some

Presbyterians, Quakers, and others formed peace societies to oppose these and all other armed conflicts. To them, the War of 1812 and the Mexican War (1845) seemed cruel and needless. Moreover, both appeared to be fought for the benefit of slaveholders, as the Southern system of labor expanded into new territories. In the three decades before the Civil War, black and white abolitionists in the North conducted a relentless, nonviolent attack on slavery. They preached, wrote, sheltered those escaping to freedom, and lobbied for and occasionally worked for racial integration.

A significant segment of abolitionists opposed all forms of violence, including war. Women first attained prominence as reformers through their participation in abolitionism, particularly the pacifist wing; one of these, Antoinette Brown Blackwell, became the first woman to be ordained a Congregational minister. Other abolitionists, such as the black leader Frederick Douglass, opposed pacifism as an undue restriction on the slaves' right to rebel. When armed rebellions were planned by groups of slaves, black preachers were usually involved, and daily resistance to slavery's violence on the part of slaves empowered by religious hope also challenged the system.

Resistance is also a theme of the Native American response to issues of war and peace. It is impossible to summarize here the long and complex Native American heritage with regard to their struggles against invasive practices. Further, Native American religions differ widely, so much so that it is inaccurate to subsume all of them under the heading "Native American Religion." Yet, two commonalities may be observed. The first is that resistance to the subjection of peoples and land by colonizers was ritually approved and celebrated in most Native American traditions. The second is that the dominant religious attitude for indigenous peoples was harmony with self, tribe, and nature. This was not a passive and interiorized harmony as in the white, Western Enlightenment tradition but a harmony that moved from a sense of the interconnectedness of all things and that included struggle and conflict.

The colonizers often justified their conflict with Native American peoples as a crusade. Righteousness was presumed to reside with the Christian and unrighteousness with the non-Christian.

The mid-nineteenth century saw a general, increased adherence to the idea of crusade. The Civil War challenged abolitionists' commitments to pacifism, and many joined the majority of the Northern public in viewing the war as a holy crusade against slavery. Sermons from ministers of almost all denominations declared that their cause was God's cause, although few noticed the irony that Southern preachers did the same.

Fiery pro-American sentiments were not unusual in the Reformed, Evangelical, and Congregational churches during the Spanish-American War (1898); although some opposition to this imperialistic venture appeared, it seemed to most Protestants to favor their efforts in foreign missions. More complex was the response to World War I on the part of the Reformed and Evangelical churches. Linked by historic and ethnic ties to Germany, the Evangelical Synod did not join the national effort to "exterminate the swinish Huns" and "make the world safe for democracy." Before and during this war, the cause of peace was actively promoted by the women's movement, then strongly organized in pursuit of women's suffrage, through the Woman's Peace Party and the Woman's International League for Peace and Freedom. One key feminist peace leader, Crystal Eastman, was the daughter of two Congregational ministers.

Chastened by the brutalities of World War I, many Protestants, including those of the traditions of the United Church of Christ, pledged in the 1920s that they would never again support a war. Some, through the Fellowship of Reconciliation (FOR) and other peace societies, expressed pacifist sentiments right up to the eve of World War II. Reinhold Niebuhr, an extremely influential theologian from the Evangelical and Reformed Church, however, resigned from FOR in 1932. Advocating "Christian realism," a modern form of the just-war doctrine, Niebuhr urged Americans in the late 1930s not to let pacifist ideals stand in the way of resistance to Hitler's tyranny.

Once the United States entered World War II, few Protestants remained pacifists. During this war, a reawakened "crusading" mentality legitimated new levels of brutality abroad, made possible by technological innovations. It also legitimated the suspension of civil rights at home as Japanese-Americans, citizens and noncitizens alike, were marched off to concentration camps. Some Congregational ministers, including several Japanese-Americans, served as chaplains in the camps, deeply concerned about the situation but rarely speaking clearly against internment. Later in the war, Japanese-Americans volunteered in large numbers to serve in the war, thus hoping to prove their "patriotism."

Following the war, Niebuhr continued his attack on pacifism, and, on the basis of his theory of Christian realism, argued for the necessity of nuclear deterrence to preserve the free world against the forces of tyranny. Along with Paul Tillich, John Bennett, Walter Horton, and others, Niebuhr endorsed this position in the Dun Commission Report, the result of a study conducted through the Federal Commission of Churches (now the National Council of the Churches of Christ).

By 1960, however, Niebuhr and Bennett among many others began to question the "balance of terror" strategy. Niebuhr wrote, "Ultimately . . . the arms race must lead to disaster. . . . That is why the old slogans of 'bargaining from strength' and 'arms to parley' and 'deterring attack by the prospect of massive retaliation' become irrelevant. A fresh approach is needed, prompted by an awareness of the common danger." John Bennett told A.J. Muste, then executive director of the Fellowship of Reconciliation, that he had come to believe that Muste's peace initiatives were prudent as well as well intentioned.

Since the 1960s, consciousness about peace and a host of other social issues came to fore. The war in Vietnam represented the first American conflict opposed by both religious and popular consensus, spawning a whole group of young Americans with a distaste for war in numbers unprecedented in U.S. history. In the same decade, black people made tremendous efforts toward racial and cultural identity, fair employment, and civil rights. Dr. Martin Luther King Jr. made a clear connection between racial injustice and war, racial justice and peace. He was one of the first black leaders to condemn the Vietnam War. Quoting a *Washington Post* figure that the U.S. government was spending $332,000 for each Vietnamese killed, King underlined the connection between that expenditure and misery in the black community. "The security we profess to seek in foreign adventures we will lose in our decaying cities. The bombs in Vietnam explode at home; they destroy the hopes and possibilities for a decent America." King knew that opposition to war was not sufficient for the existence of peace. "It is not enough to say, 'We must not wage war.' It is necessary to love peace and sacrifice for it."

Asians, Hispanics, and Native Americans to varying degrees pursued parallel paths, while women of all races began to make similar efforts toward empowerment and full equality. Together, these efforts lifted up issues of social, racial, and economic justice before the American people as a whole.

In the years since the war, much public attention has turned toward the arms race and the prospect of nuclear annihilation, and several U.S. and European churches, including the United Church of Christ, have adopted strong positions on disarmament. Other groups have promoted peace and justice along different lines. Pacific Islanders, for example, have resisted the use of Palau, the Marianas, and other islands for military bases, the disposal of nuclear wastes, and target practice. And scores of U.S. churches, recognizing the repressiveness of the U.S.-supported regimes in Guatemala and El Salvador, have begun to offer sanctuary to refugees denied refuge by the United States government and its policies.

Despite all these initiatives, our times have been marked by divergent attitudes towards questions of peace and justice. The last four years have seen an erosion of civil rights and social programs, a burgeoning military budget, the rehabilitation of the Vietnam War, and rising U.S. intervention in conflicts in the Middle East and Central America. Our nation and our world—as well as our churches—stand at a crossroads. As has been noted, our histories—secular and religious—bring us to no unequivocal position; our churches and our nation have taken a variety of positions from pacifism to crusade. Recognizing the diversity inherent in our traditions, we must now ask how to be most faithful as makers of peace and justice in this new age.

Christian Traditions and the New Historical Situation

Theology and Christian ethics always emerge in specific historical situations. This is no less true for Christian thinking about war and peace. The concepts of holy war and crusade, for example, come out of the historical situations in which Jews and Christians were out of power or not in control of the lands they were considering taking over. Just-war theory developed as theologians reflected on what advice Christians might give rulers who were defending territory against what were perceived as barbaric outsiders. Pacifism emerged in historical situations where Christians felt politically powerless but did not want to be in power because of their conviction that the emergence of God's reign made the political process irrelevant.

Christians need, therefore, to examine the historical situation today as they pursue a theology of Just Peace. At least five factors are dramatically changing the way Christians view issues of war and peace in this time and place. Two of these factors are particularly dominant and influence the other three.

QUALITATIVELY NEW WEAPONS

One fact that represents a break with the past is the massive technological revolution in weapons. The awesome power of nuclear weapons was revealed when the United States used the atomic bomb in Hiroshima and Nagasaki in 1945. Some who participated in making the bomb and in deciding to use it came to the conclusion that such a weapon should never be used again after the horrors of those bombings became apparent. With the creation of the atomic bomb, the institution of war changed forever.

In the late 1940s and 1950s there was wide public debate about what would follow, now that the historic meaning of war was outmoded. What followed was an arms race in the name of deterrence. For forty years, the superpowers—and today the lesser powers as well—have devoted massive portions of their national treasure and genius to the development of weapons that dwarf the original atomic bombs in their destructive power. The doctrine of deterrence—superpowers threatening each other with such destructive force that neither dares go to war against the other—has produced a kind of stasis. It has also transferred the institution of war into Third World countries, where well over one hundred have occurred since 1945, many spurred on by the indirect conflict between the superpowers.

The spiral of armament and counterarmament is a phenomenon that seems to fit unobtrusively into people's everyday notions of the progress of technology and business. But once again we have recognized that we are dealing with more than the mere improvement of weapons. We are witnessing a new historical reality: our weapons are now giving us the capacity to end human history and all life forms on earth. We face global suicide. Because war no longer means what it used to mean, just war and crusade no longer fit the new context.

North-South Conflict

Polarization between rich and poor is not new. Oppression is not new. What is new is the global nature of this division wherein the poverty of the South is directly related to the wealth of the North. Over the past two hundred years, colonial structures have transferred wealth from poorer countries to richer countries. These structures are now solidly in place, creating not just a "developed" North but an "underdeveloped" South.

For centuries, the notions of "just war" and "deterrence" were generated by and found their context of meaning in Europe and North America. They related principally to the balance of power within the northern hemisphere.

This northern balance of power is now being challenged by the Third World. People in the Third World, victims of the wars between the East and West that have been transferred to the southern hemisphere and of the structural injustice and power plays of capitalist and socialist countries, are insisting on new ways to understand war and peace. The struggle for the just distribution of wealth and the self-determination of peoples is more and more directed against the developed world. Third World peoples see the struggle between the East and West as a threat to their future, as a ploy to control their natural and human resources.

The day is rapidly approaching when wars even in the Third World will be outmoded, just as war in the North has become outmoded. The weapons revolution will soon provide the means of mass destruction to all nations and peoples. The developed countries will no longer be able to dictate to the underdeveloped countries on the basis of weapons, and the logic of the East-West conflict will no longer apply. War is being redefined in this generation.

The conflict between North and South, rich and poor, is not just geographical. The creation of national-security states around the world is also at the expense of the poor within such nations. Because their governments are committed to producing weaponry, the poor who live within national-security states are denied food and jobs and housing. They are also denied access to the power and status of those running the national-security systems. The rich and powerful, East and West, North and South, keep the poor in place by frightening them with the threat of an external enemy against whom society must be organized in ways that justify repression and injustice at home.

Ethical and theological attempts to offer guidance on how to resolve conflict and achieve justice must be developed, based on the new context of weapons of mass destruction and structural injustice and oppression on a global scale. Three more factors also shape the new context.

EAST-WEST CONFLICT

In 1917, the Communist revolution in Russia created a new historical situation. Marxist analysts see this event as a critical historical transformation. Because Western democracies do not agree with the Marxist view, the world has settled into a permanent state of polarization.

The Cold War has become a seemingly permanent war. Peace is not perceived as really possible by either side, nor is reconciliation. Each side projects the necessity of defeating the other side. In the context of the new weapons, the stakes rise to qualitatively new levels. Nuclear technology is used to claim world superiority and ascendancy, creating the global myth that the future of the world rests on U.S. and Soviet relationships.

The historical situation is shaped by those in the power structures of East and West who seem willing to use all means of nuclear destruction to keep their own ideology, national identity, and way of life intact and ascendant. What are clearly human constructs are elevated in value over God's creation and the totality of God's people and creatures.

29

While the power elites of both East and West project the image that the global East–West struggle is for the sake of supreme values of equality, justice, and democracy, the poor and the oppressed perceive and experience the ideology of East and West as one more tool of oppression used to mask the power and national claims of the superpowers.

Deteriorating National and World Order

Just at the time when the East–West and North–South struggles are intensifying and the threats to use weapons of mass destruction increase, national and international structures of law and diplomacy are proving ever less capable of creating and preserving world order. There is a growing sense of alienation from governments and states; they are seen as ineffective pawns of larger but less visible historical processes.

As nations continue to rely on stockpiles of weaponry for security and grow less able to produce any lasting and real security, the response by both large and small nations is to increase the commitment to nationalism and resist power being shifted to international authorities. The superpowers hold on to what power they have, and newly liberated nations cling to the concept of the nation-state as the only means they have found for national liberation in such chaotic and oppressive times. The concept of common security is devalued as the commitment to nationalism increases.

Apocalyptic Despair

The new historical situation is causing many people the world over to anticipate in fear a destruction that seems guaranteed. Some fear nuclear holocaust. Some experience hopeless oppression. Some Christians believe that God will use nuclear weapons to destroy a godless world. Some children and youth do not see the point of growing up. They are human beings living under the condition of mass destruction through their loss of hope and vitality, through the rigidity of a life constantly defended, and through a devotion to the means of self-destruction. Their fear already realizes in the present the threatened future. Such despair centers economic and political power in the national-security state, heightening the possibility of extermination rather than offering constructs for human well-being.

Hope for real security, based upon the common need for justice and reconciliation, is lost amid the despair.

Deterrence

The meaning of the new historical situation in which we live comes to a focus in the doctrine of deterrence, which world leaders have claimed to be the doctrine that guarantees a future for the world. The church in general (including the United Church of Christ) gave oral sanction to this doctrine as the arms race got underway in the 1950s. On January 31, 1958, for example, the United Church of Christ Council for Christian Social Action passed a resolution that said in part:

> The free nations are thus presented with a situation in which military weapons equal, or superior, to those possessed by the Communist power appear necessary as a deterrent to aggressive military designs, while at the same time the prospects of large-scale use of weapons has become intolerable.

Peace, justice, and freedom will not be served in the present situation by a decision on the part of the United States and its allies not to maintain weapons approximately equal to those possessed by the Soviet Union.

Catholic and Protestant churches during this time gave sanction to nuclear deterrence only as a threat, not for wide-scale use, and only so long as serious efforts were under way to achieve disarmament and a new global order where conflict could be resolved nonviolently.

In the twenty-five years since these stands were taken, it is clear that insufficient progress has been made toward disarmament or a new global order. In fact, the arms race has increased considerably.

It has become clear that the moral advice of the church that sanctioned the threat to use nuclear weapons but not their actual use is failed policy and failed theology. A threat is only real or credible when everyone is convinced that the threat will be carried out. In the late 1970s and early 1980s, the U.S. government began to suspect that its threat to use nuclear weapons had become less credible. The intentional decision was made to assure everyone that the U.S. nuclear threat was indeed real.

It is partly in response to this renewed threat that the peace movement has gained such energy in the 1980s and churches have begun to rethink their sanction of deterrence. Important to this rethinking is the fact that weaponry has now been developed to the point where defensive and offensive weapons cannot be distinguished.

As both sides move toward first-strike capability, where nuclear-tipped missiles take only six to twelve minutes to fly from launch to target, the hair-trigger nature of the situation with reliance on computers for "launch on warning" creates a condition of instability.

Deterrence may have had some justification as an interim ethic, to gain time for the development of a genuine and real security based upon a more stable international order of justice and peace. The time of its possible usefulness has passed. From the perspective of the poor in Third World countries, who have suffered not only the continued oppression of an unjust global order but also the displacement caused by wars between East and West that have been carried out on their soil and with their lives, the doctrine of deterrence loses any moral justification.

The United Church of Christ must constantly keep its historical and present situation in view when searching for the resources to create a peace theology.

3.

TURNING TOWARD
A JUST PEACE

The Biblical Vision of Shalom

THE BIBLE PRESENTS a vision of Just Peace. It is the story of God's people struggling for peace in many different situations and in many different ways.

The basic biblical vision is the vision of shalom, which means "peace." But shalom means peace in a much fuller sense than the English language conveys. Shalom means wholeness, healing, justice, righteousness, equality, unity, freedom, and community. Shalom is a vision of all people whole, well, and one, and of all nature whole, well, and one. For this reason the authors have chosen to translate *shalom* as "Just Peace" to bring out in a fresh way the uniqueness of the biblical vision of shalom as a challenge to our times.

From the moment of God's creation in Genesis through the promise of covenant to Abraham, to the unity that is given in Christ Jesus, God's will for creation and for all people is shalom.

The all-embracing character of shalom is evident in the following passage:

> I will make with them a covenant of shalom and banish wild beasts from the land, so that they may dwell securely in the wilderness and sleep in the woods. And I will make them and the places round about my hill a blessing; and I will send down the showers in their season; they shall be showers of blessing. And the trees of the field shall yield their fruit, and the earth shall yield its increase, and they shall be secure in their land. . . . They shall no more be a prey to the nations, nor shall the beasts of the land devour them; they shall dwell securely, and none shall make them afraid. And I will provide for them plantations of shalom.
> —Ezekiel 34:25–29

The very extravagance of the vision is characteristic of descriptions of shalom. Not only does blessing upon blessing come to the human community, but the human community is surrounded and at peace with the land, its fruits, and its creatures. Isaiah is best known for expressing the shalom vision as the termination not merely of human enmity but also of enmity in all creation.

> The wolf shall dwell with the lamb, and the leopard shall lie down with the kid, and the calf and the lion and the fatling together, and a little child shall lead them. The cow and the bear shall feed; their young shall lie down together; and the lion shall eat straw like the ox. The sucking child shall play over the hole of the asp, and the weaned child shall put a hand on the adder's den.
> —Isaiah 11:6–8

A world where children and snakes are in harmony is the time of creation when the peace and joy of the Sabbath (Genesis 2:1–4a) is present, and all "lie down and none make afraid." The most familiar Sabbath blessing ends by asking God to look upon the human community and give shalom (Numbers 6:26).

The absence of shalom is expressed in the disorder of creation and the disordering of the human community. Social and economic inequalities, political oppression and strife are a direct affront to God's will that the human community dwell in shalom. When shalom is broken by oppression, God, through the leaders of the people, strives to break the bonds of human enslavement and establish shalom again.

In Isaiah this theme is fully expanded, and shalom is inextricably bound to justice and righteousness. Doing justice becomes a central way of expressing fidelity to God and God's will for the human community.

The Year of the Jubilee in the Old Testament, which was one more way of moving to break the bonds of oppression and to reestablish the conditions of shalom, is a theme that is picked up in the New Testament as central to the purpose and ministry of Jesus:

> The Spirit of the Lord is upon me who has annointed me to preach good news to the poor. The Lord has sent me to proclaim release to the captives and recovering of sight to the blind, to set at liberty those who are oppressed, to proclaim the acceptable year of the Lord.
> —Luke 4:18–19

In the New Testament, shalom is the fulfillment of the promises made to Israel. Christ is therefore the author of shalom. In the first two Gospels, the message of shalom is the message that God's reign on earth has begun. In Luke, Jesus is pictured as proclaiming the shalom of God through both word and deed.

The Epistles, which use the word for peace even more frequently than the Gospels, tend to focus on shalom in the church rather than in the world and look to the church as the first fruits of God's gift of shalom. Paul speaks of those who are "in Christ" as new creatures or new creations. The theme of unity is particularly strong: Christ is our shalom who has made us all one and who has broken down all dividing walls of hostility (Ephesians 2). The shalom that is given to the church in Christ is of course seen by Paul as God's strategy for the much larger transformation into an inclusive shalom for all creation: the church is the "first fruits" of a more inclusive transformation.

Yet other voices also exist within the biblical corpus. Violent and vindictive imagery occurs. Yahweh is pictured as a holy warrior who demands complete destruction of Israel's enemies, and Saul is chastened for not following God's command to "slay all the men, women, and children of the Amalekites."

The New Testament contains its share of ambiguous passages. John the Baptist does not try to dissuade soldiers from military service; he merely exhorts them not to complain about their wages. Jesus clearly did not shy away from conflict, and did not always take the path of reconciliation. The same Jesus who says, "Turn the other cheek," and "Resist not evil," also says, "I have not come to bring peace, but a sword," and "If my kingdom were of this world, my servants would fight." Jesus used force, if not violence, to remove money changers from the temple.

If the biblical vision of shalom is clear: lions dwelling with lambs, swords into plowshares, nations not studying war, the path to this vision seems less clear. There is no foreign policy blueprint in the Bible. There is the story of a God who seeks shalom, Just Peace, and who stirs up the people, time and again, to create the conditions of a Just Peace and to take fresh initiatives to bring unity, reconciliation, forgiveness, and justice.

Voices from the Struggle for Liberation

As Christians we find ourselves in the midst of just such a stirring of God's will for shalom, Just Peace, today. Just Peace identifies the church's vocation today as actively witnessing to the good news of God's presence and promise of justice and peace on earth. At the same time, it is a reaffirmation of a powerful tradition, biblical and postbiblical: the prophetic linking of justice and peace and the gospel emphasis on the present and coming realm of God. The concept of a Just Peace brings together the imperatives and promises of justice and peace. It addresses the whole of life—personal and social, spiritual and political, attitudinal and structural. The theological task is to explore the meaning of Just Peace for the life of the church today.

If as Christians we are to discern God's will for today, we must attend to the coming together of this key biblical imperative of shalom and the work of those engaged in the vocations of creating a more just and peaceful world. We start from the recognition that God's word of Just Peace today is heard most powerfully in the voices of those who have largely borne and still bear the burden of social, economic, and political oppression. We affirm that the biblical vision of shalom is held up to the church today by those who have been and are oppressed: the poor, people of color, women of all classes and colors, gay and lesbian people, the old, and the victims of crime and war.

It is nevertheless important to emphasize that the struggle for liberation is broader than that. There are those who have to some extent enjoyed the fruits of privilege but who are now seeking liberation from their complicity in oppression and unjust privilege. To a certain extent, all people are caught in the bondage of violence and death that characterizes the structures of privilege and oppression. We are all stunted and imprisoned by complicity, arrogance, indifference, and fear. The world cannot be divided into "good people" and "bad people," oppressed and oppressor. Indeed, most of us, perhaps all of us in the United Church of Christ, live out lives of both oppression and privilege.

And yet, even the struggle for liberation from privilege can be corrupted by privilege. It is always necessary to remind ourselves and to be reminded by others that the privileged who are engaged in the struggle for liberation must continuously test whether their engagement ignores or reflects the insights and revelations of the dispossessed. We must acknowledge the need for insights from the previously silent oppressed because that is where God is speaking to us today.

The biblical vision of shalom, Just Peace, has enabled us to see God's promise, God's decision to be present with the poor and dispossessed. It is the work of the church to listen to the voice of God in the voices of the dispossessed and to be present where God has chosen to be present.

ECONOMIC RELATIONS

Amongst those who have been deprived of the means to live decently are those who have become conscious that their condition is neither accidental nor the inevitable by-product of "market forces." They have exposed the "market fallacy," the notion that all economic matters must be left to the free play of the market, which should exist in isolation from the limitations of ethical criteria.

The discovery of those who have not benefited from the free play of market forces is that these forces are relatively new phenomena, theories created to account for the practice in industrialized societies of the reduction of human life to production and consumption.

The shalom vision, each person under his or her own vine and fig tree, represents an older view of economics as the allocation of what it takes to live. Economics traditionally defined means, in Greek, *oikos*, "house" or "household," and *nomos*, "manager." It is the job of the economist to manage the household so that each has the means to live.

God is the householder, the good manager, who has provided sufficiently for the household. The stewards, however, have not seen to it that the distribution of the goods of the household is fair. The voices of the children deprived of bread are the voice of God confronting the stewards for their unjust management.

Free market economic theories are, on the contrary, not directed toward the more equal distribution of goods but toward the accumulation of goods by fewer and fewer individuals and corporations. This is especially true in the economic relations of recent years. Since the mid-1970s, the distribution of income has widened in the United States. Between 1979 and 1983, a major study just completed by the Urban Institute indicates that the average family income fell 2 percent. But among the poorest fifth of the population it dropped 9.4 percent, while among the richest fifth it fell only .5 percent. World figures vary greatly. Some countries have increased income distribution toward equity: On the one hand, Japan, for example, has moved toward more equal income distribution. Brazil, on the other hand, has experienced a gross widening of income for rich and poor.

The point, however, is that these economic changes are not inevitable, nor are they always desirable. They are not inevitable because they are the constructions of those who benefit from inequality. Those who have benefited from these economic constructions have an investment in regarding inequality as natural, inevitable, and unchangeable. As poor people have discovered themselves to be capable of affecting their world, however, they have come to understand that these market forces are not fate but realities that can be named, understood, and changed. Other systems can be constructed that promote more equitable distribution. Recently the American Catholic bishops have written that Americans need to extend their understanding of political democracy to economic democracy.

What is called "free market" economics is not an equitable pattern because not only does it legitimate injustice for those who are deprived of the means to live, but it threatens the survival of the whole household. When a smaller and smaller minority of the world's people has access to two thirds of its resources, the ties of dependency and exploitation increase daily.

The exploitation, enslavement, and genocide of Native Americans and Africans has been followed by political and economic dependency and impoverishment of most of Central and South America, India, and the other Asian countries. When land that once provided at least a subsistence living grows crops primarily for export, business may boom in the midst of starvation. In the Dominican Republic, for instance, in the 1970s sugar cane production rose dramatically while more and more Dominicans starved. Similarly, during the drought in the Sahel, which continues today, large cotton crops for export have been flourishing while the indigenous people starve.

This structure of exploitation and oppression reaches back to the United States, not only in profits to U.S. corporations, but in the layoffs of U.S. workers who cannot produce as cheaply as those elsewhere. It reaches even farther by reinforcing U.S. commitment to military expenditures to keep quiet restive countries where we have huge economic interests. Imperialism is a significant source of poverty, oppression, and hostility in the rest of the world; it also weakens and destabilizes the possibilities of a Just Peace within our own nation. As we increase our military spending, we drain money away from social programs and add an impetus to the arms race, which in turn aggravates tensions with the Soviet Union.

STRUCTURES OF VIOLENCE

In the voices of those who have suffered deprivation is heard the voice of God protesting the presence of many forms of violence in the human community. In this voice the deceptive faces of violence have been stripped of their masks and the forms of violence exposed in all their many complexities.

The root of the problem as seen "from below" is one of power and its equitable distribution. The World Council of Churches Consultation on Racism meeting at Notting Hill, England, in 1969 stated that the center of the problem was "not simply that of violence versus nonviolence, but the use of power for the powerful and the need of power for the powerless." Nonwhite members of the commission in particular had opened the eyes of the world church to the fact that the really decisive question is not the question of violence—especially since the concept of "violence" can be widened to cover indirect forms of pressure—but the question of the justification of the power, the consequent limits of power, and the fact that power can become unjust and tyrannical.

"Indirect forms of pressure" is an important insight. Violence can be both overt, as in bombing in war, or covert, as in the structures of racism, sexism or homophobia, which maim and cripple human lives without a bomb ever falling. As well as overt, physical expressions, violence can be built into the apparently peaceful operations of a society. Lack of educational opportunity, poor housing conditions, barriers to equal employment, condescension, as well as terror and other less subtle forms of psychological numbing, can cripple human life.

When covert structures of violence are challenged, overt, physical violence is often the result, as those in power seek to retain their dominance. Resistance to violent repression cannot summarily be dismissed as always wrong by those who have never experienced the deep-seated impotence of those who see violent resistance as their only means of defense. Those who are not in violently repressive situations can no longer determine how revolutionary people, in El Salvador for example, should defend themselves. Rather, their task is to work to end violent repression and make resistance of any sort unnecessary.

SOCIAL RELATIONS AND POWER

The dispossessed of every culture have a direct experience of what it means to be out of power, to be powerless. Their voices are the voice of God,

44

challenging the prevailing stereotype of power as strength that is either superior or inferior to that of another. They offer another model of power, as relational. Power-as-relation resides between or among people, not simply in any one person.

In this model, power is increased as it is shared. It is not competitive. Where there is consent, there is free-flowing action, the accomplishing of intention. In the lives of the dispossessed who have organized to protest their dispossession, these new forms of human community can be glimpsed, despite the deformations of terrorism. Movements such as the Basic Christian Communities in Latin America evidence the presence of God moving in their midst as a power that binds instead of divides, a power that increases as it is shared.

Responsibility

Because God is moving in the world, possibilities open up and change can take place. God is active where some who have had relatively more power and privilege have heard the cries of the poor and have experienced a conversion to the cause of the poor. They have begun to be converted to the view that they bear a great responsibility to end poverty, militarism, and imperialism.

Together those who seek to be responsive to God's presence today in the movement toward shalom are also saying to those who continue to aid these spirals of violence, "Basta! Enough! If you will not accept responsibility, you are to be held accountable and restrained so that others can be given the power to act." This needs to be said in terms of massive voter registration and the selection of those who will take responsibility. If that fails, it is time to say, "Enough!" in acts of dissent, noncooperation, and civil disobedience.

Responsibility means that the dispossessed should not bear alone the burden for ending the violence that is visited upon them. It is the responsibility of those who have access to power to change the conditions that make violent acts seem necessary. If, for instance, the world is to avoid revolutionary violence, those in power need to work to eliminate the oppression that provokes it. If society is to bring an end to the violence of abortion, we should do so by making provision for children and the choice to bear children in ways that do not penalize women. Just Peace, therefore, is rooted in the God-given responsibility of human beings to create a just and equitable human community.

Taking responsibility for ending violence means a major shift away from resolving conflict with either overt or covert violence to resolving conflict with means that are open and honest and that avoid violence. There must be a major emphasis on imaginative and creative means for social change that empower and build solidarity in such ways that change becomes nearly inevitable.

Certainly violence was not a part of Jesus' vision of the reign of God nor of his own life in any sustained fashion. Our vocation as Christians is to take responsibility in our time, as Jesus did in his time, to be as clear as we can about the promise of shalom, Just Peace, and to act—in peace and justice, for peace and justice.

Friendship

The arms race is a kind of bondage. Bondage is also the continuation of patterns of racism and sexism; of prejudice and privilege; of fear, suspicion, and hostility; of action and reaction and retaliation. Bondage is what is happening in Lebanon and Nicaragua and in the United States between economic institutions and the poor, on and on with no release, no real justice, no peace.

God's forgiveness is what begins truly to set us free from this bondage. Forgiveness is necessary if we are to move from death to life. Sometimes, to forgive is to accept, but forgiveness does not equal acceptance. Forgiveness is not passive. God did not forgive the world by simply sighing and accepting sin. The story is quite different. It is the story of Christmas, of incarnation, of challenge to the status quo and suffering and dying and being resurrected—all very active events. Forgiveness is setting free, cutting away that which binds us to the past, whether it be our internal past, the past of a relationship, or the imprisoning history of groups and nations.

God's forgiveness creates the conditions of Just Peace. Forgiveness is a sign of the presence of God the Holy Spirit moving through the creative and courageous forgiveness of peacemakers as they take the risk of applying new approaches that allow for new responses. Forgiveness is taking risks and trying new approaches that permit change to occur. Forgiveness is deciding not to play the game of the arms race any longer, thereby creating a whole new set of possibilities for international relationships. It is beginning to think of the Soviets as not-yet friends and figuring out how to evoke their friendship and disarm their fear and suspicion.

Forgiveness makes friendship possible. Friendship, in contrast to paternalism and some other kinds of love, includes a relation of respect and loyalty. It is also a relation of challenge and confrontation and forgiveness and the painful move to reconciliation. Friendship illumines the reality and the role of conflict, and it can be a source of growth and insight. Friends work hard at moving through conflict. Friendship and peace do not mean the absence of conflict; friends acknowledge the inevitability and value of honest, open, and nonviolent conflict and pledge themselves to work through conflict toward changed perception and resolution.

To think of Just Peace in terms of friendship does not mean that everyone should become friends with everyone else in the world or that governments should necessarily all love one another. It does mean that many of the qualities found in friendship—forgiveness and loyalty and trust and respect—are deeply necessary for peace. Justice and power make reconciliation possible, but forgiveness and loyalty make it actual. Justice and power need to be expressed in policy and action, but unless the principles of friendship are similarly expressed, justice and power will never be secure, and peace will never become a reality.

This means that, in addition to structural change, a transformation of values must also occur. Values such as competition, victory, being number one, being better than someone else, traditional definitions of honor, and the acceptance of lying in the public sphere are, from the perspective of a Just Peace, all destructive, oppressive, and dehumanizing. These are among the values that sanction and maintain hierarchy. They are preeminently among the values that sanction and maintain sexism.

Once again, new voices bring important messages, specifically women's voices. Some women have written and spoken of the values of nurturing, of reconciling, of listening to others, of caring for physical and emotional needs and well-being—values that have been forced on certain groups and at the same time been devalued. These values remain the most humane and central for becoming friends, for moving toward a Just Peace, and indeed, for setting free the reality and the power of the gospel. In these women's voices is heard the voice of God, raising up these qualities to the service of the human community. The voice of God in all these voices from the under side of history urges Christians to begin the task of a theological foundation for the Just Peace Church.

4.   THEOLOGICAL FOUNDATIONS OF THE JUST PEACE CHURCH

THE JUST PEACE church is one of the first fruits of an inclusive transformation of the whole earth and its people in the direction of shalom. Attending closely to our sources in history, the Bible, and present–day life, we Christians must take responsibility for the role of the church in the movement of the whole world toward peace and wholeness. Our responsibility as a denomination is to be theologically accountable in our identity as a Just Peace church and faithful in the work of Just Peace.

   The following is not a full exposition of all the topics to be covered in a peace theology. Instead, the authors have tried to touch on some of the main doctrines of the church: creation, sin, the Christ, the Spirit, the church, church and state, hope. They explore how these doctrines might be developed as the theology of a Just Peace is further explored. As the United Church of Christ continues to struggle with becoming a Just Peace church, the theological implications of Just Peace need to be elaborated and developed.

Creation: Covenant as Friendship

In the beginning, humanity was shaped by God. Human beings are witnesses to the creativity of God, the desire of God to create and not destroy. This was declared good because we were created to be with God. God does not want to be alone. God makes room for humanity. We are thus created both with and in God by virtue of our creation by God. We are inseparably related to God.

The creation narratives of the scriptures are not in conflict with science. They describe the creation as the beginning of history. The creation anticipates what is to come: a lifelong relationship between human beings and God. God and the people of God move through history together. The bond between them deepens and strengthens over time.

In the early years of their history together, God offered the people a chance to break with the Egyptian Pharaoh and his idols of sand and to take a risk in the wilderness. Though enslaved and oppressed in Egypt, the people of God are brought out of Egypt, out of slavery, and their lives are forever changed. But God is changed too. God agrees to become their God and to abide with them. "I will make a covenant of peace with them; it shall be an everlasting covenant with them; and I will bless them and multiply them, and will set my sanctuary in the midst of them for evermore [Ezek. 37:26]."

In entering into covenant with them, God has freely chosen to abide in the midst of them. The covenant of God with the people is a self-chosen risk on God's part in which God limits divine freedom for the sake of a true partnership with humanity. Covenant represents a form of governance of the world that is a sharing of power, not an exercise of tyrannical authority.

This is why the marriage metaphor keeps recurring to describe the relationship of God and the people of God. While sometimes these biblical images have been used to identify the male role with the role of God, the biblical metaphor of marriage can be interpreted not to signify the subordination of women but the intense involvement of God and the people. The real content of the metaphor is the learning to bond with one another—as difficult in human relations as in the divine–human relation. Our continuing encounter with the scriptures in present history makes new interpretations necessary if we are really to hear the text in the present.

The book of Hosea contains a lament of God over the unfaithfulness of Israel. Israel is imaged as God's wife. This represents the risk God is taking. In marriage one never quite knows how things are going to turn out. What is certain, though, is that the marriage will be different from anyone's expectations, and both partners will be changed by it.

This understanding challenges the concept of a solitary, self-sufficient God, who comes into covenant with everything settled. Instead, things are decided as the relationship goes along. God tells Hosea to return to his wife just as God turns again to Israel and renews the covenant, despite having said in anger, "You are not my people, and I am not your God [Hos. 1:9]."

> And I will make for you a covenant on that day with the beasts of the field, the birds of the air, and the creeping things of the ground; and I will abolish the bow, the sword, and war from the land; and I will make you lie down in safety. And I will betroth you to me in righteousness and in justice, in steadfast love, and in mercy. I will betroth you to me in faithfulness; and you shall know the Sovereign.
>
> —Hosea 2:18–20

Hosea depicts not a triumphant God, who does not get involved with the people, but a God who makes peace through participating in the lives of the people and risking even hurt and rejection.

A current way of describing such a relationship is with another metaphor, that of friendship. In the scriptures, God's bonding with humanity is also described as friendship.

> But you, Israel, my servant, Jacob, whom I have chosen, the offspring of Abraham, my friend . . .
>
> —Isaiah 41:8

The description of God's relationship with humanity as friendship expresses mutuality, maturity, cooperation, responsibility, and reciprocity. This relationship of friendship, of covenant, brings about shalom, the well–being that is peace, when the weapons of war are swept off the earth and all creatures lie down together without fear.

Furthermore, covenantal fidelity is not confined to human relationship to God. It is the totality of God's abiding with the people of God as they keep covenant with one another. As people living in friendship with God, we come to recognize the inseparable connection between knowing God and doing justice to one another.

> Did not your ancestors eat and drink and do justice and righteousness? Then it was well. They judged the cause of the poor and needy; then it was well. Is this not to know me? says God, the Sovereign one.
>
> —Jeremiah 22:15-16

The Just Peace church is rooted in this understanding of covenant. God's move to bond with us in friendship opens up the possibility that such friendship is possible on earth.

Sin: The Refusal of God's Friendship

The biblical writers are never romantic about shalom. Those who have continued to struggle for peace and justice throughout human history know as well that Just Peace does not come naturally or smoothly. They are clear that humanity finds many ways to refuse the shalom vision and to turn away from God's will for human history.

One of the ways the community refuses the reality of Just Peace is to be, as the Latin American theologian Gustavo Gutierrez has said, a "liar society." Injustice, greed, and preparation for war are mislabeled "peacekeeping." But what is kept is not peace, but injustice and greed. The prophet Jeremiah did not mince words in identifying the sin of denying shalom.

> *For from the least to the greatest of them, every one is greedy for unjust gain; and from prophet to priest, every one deals falsely. They have healed the wounds of my people lightly, Saying, "Shalom, Shalom," when there is no shalom.*
> —Jeremiah 6:13–14; 8:11;
> cf. Ezekiel 13:10, 16; Amos 6:1–6

Just Peace is a responsibility for the powerful. They are held accountable when prosperity is a possibility only for a few. The well–being of a small segment is not Just Peace but is in fact the refusal to see the shalom vision in all its breadth.

Another way in which the community can refuse Just Peace, shalom, is to mortgage the future for an uneasy security in the present. Going heavily into debt to buy armaments to protect the disproportionate prosperity of a few is a related refusal of shalom.

Deficit spending has been sanctioned in contemporary economic theory, but its pernicious effects were known long before the theories of the twentieth century. Isaiah records a story of King Hezekiah, who was willing to mortgage the future of his people for excess in the present, saying to himself, "There will be shalom and security in my days [Isa. 39:8]." The prophet condemns such a narrow understanding of the well-being that is shalom. (See also Jeremiah 31:29, 30; Ezekiel 18:2.) Just Peace is not limited to a few people or to only one generation. The deficits incurred in the United States today to pay for arms buildup decrease shalom for some people through inflation and joblessness. But they also mortgage the Just Peace of the future, condemning the future generations to pay for the spending sprees of the present.

Another way to refuse the broad and deep vision of Just Peace is to confine Just Peace to religious rituals. Again it is Jeremiah who is clear in criticizing the people for finding the temple a quick and easy way to shalom (Jeremiah 7:1–10). Jesus as well condemned going through the motions of religious ritual without connecting ritual to ethical conduct (Matthew 15:1–20).

The shalom vision that the authors have translated "Just Peace" is so comprehensive that there is a great temptation to try to manage its challenge and identify shalom with a particular technology or economic theory or present gratification or even a religious ritual. Over and over through human history people have rebelled against participating in the reign of God and have refused to see and do God's will for human life.

Christ: Jesus and the Power for Change

Even though generation after generation has refused Just Peace with God, we have no cause for despair. The advent of Christ is the joyous seal of our friendship with God, a friendship described in the Old Testament as a time when God speaks peace to the people and "steadfast love and faithfulness will meet; righteousness and peace will kiss each other. Faithfulness will spring up from the ground, and righteousness will look down from the sky [Ps. 85:10–11]."

Jesus, who is our peace (Ephesians 1:14), really changed human history so that it is possible to overcome the sin of refusing shalom. Jesus, when he was on earth, participated in the reign of God in a visible, tangible way. Jesus himself performed visible signs of forgiveness and healing that made manifest that the Just Peace vision was no longer merely future but also present. Through his death on the cross and his resurrection, Jesus made it possible for Christians to participate in a real way in Just Peace. The church strives to continue to live that concrete manifestation.

But, Christians generally have looked at the coming of Christ, and hence the role of the church, in ways that are not so concrete. In one view, they have seen the coming of Christ simply as a transaction between God and Christ alone in which the sacrifice of Jesus causes God to forgive humankind's sin and offer redemption. In another view they have seen the coming of Christ in terms of personal interaction between Christ and each believer. In this view, the individual turns to God by appropriating Christ's sacrifice for the self. But in either view, the power Christ brings actually to change the world is turned away from the world and frozen in a transaction that is outside history.

It is essential for the church to maintain the tension between proclaiming the real change that Christ did make in human history, opening up through his death and resurrection the possibility of humanity's turning to God, without at the same time turning this power for change into "a noun," as Hugo Assman, another Latin American theologian, has phrased it. The power for change is not a "noun," that is, something static, but a "verb," something in which we actively participate. The work of Christ to change the world and bring it closer to God makes possible our work as we continue to bring about Just Peace.

What the work of Christ means is that the coming of Christ is more than placating God's anger at human sin and more than an individual's heart being turned to faith. While it includes both of these things, it also means that the coming of Christ really changed human history. Humanity can overcome sin, create Just Peace. It also means that this power for change is useless if human beings do not bond together to participate in changing the world. Christ's power becomes tangible through our bonding with one another.

Today, one of the strongest images of the atonement, a word that means the reconciliation brought about by Christ's sacrifice on the cross, is the suffering and pain of the oppressed. Jesus, identified in earthly life as one who was a friend of tax collectors and sinners (Matthew 11:19), acted out the message that the power to change the world comes from human solidarity.

Table fellowship shows this clearly. People eat with their friends, those with whom they have a close relationship. Jesus, who ate with the unclean, the outcast, and those in despised professions, showed that the power to change the world comes through human bonding with the despised.

Friendship was an important part of Jesus' life. But it is clear that by friendship Jesus does not mean the easy camaraderie of clubs, social organizations, or even some churches. Jesus speaks of the love of those willing to lay down their lives for their friends (John 15:13).

As a Just Peace church, members embody not a Christ who touched history only tangentially but a Christ fully engaged in human events as the fulfillment of God's promise to befriend the people. The church is thus a real countervailing power to those forces that perpetuate human enmity, that divide and destroy human community.

The Holy Spirit: Advocate for Justice

This power for change is still available to Christians and we do not have to act alone. Jesus promised us that we would not be alone in history, that we would not be orphaned. Jesus promised God would send another, the Spirit of Truth (John 14:16).

"Comforter" and "Sustainer" are other translations of the Greek word for Spirit usually found in John 14. These translations reflect a view of the Holy Spirit as "persuader." The Spirit is deemed to act individualistically, privately, and indirectly.

To comfort, to sustain are actions that complement the status quo and help people to adjust to their problems. While there are times of personal crisis when the Holy Spirit does come to us to comfort and sustain, the work of the Spirit is not limited to these actions. The Holy Spirit is as fully immersed in the struggles of human history as was the one by whom the Spirit was sent, Jesus the Christ. To limit the work of the Holy Spirit only to "comforting" and "sustaining" is to reflect a view of history as harmonious and untroubled. Yet,

Christians view history as troubled, an arena of conflict, of struggle, in which the hegemony of the "principalities and powers" has been ended by Christ, but in which we must still struggle finally to defeat them.

The work of the Spirit includes a genuine effort at making right what has been wrong. Thus, an important part of the work of the Holy Spirit is witness and proclamation, even confrontation with those sinful rejections of the vision of Just Peace and the attempts to subvert its establishment.

In this struggle to defeat the power ranged against the shalom vision, however, we Christians undercut our own purposes if we do not make forgiveness our first act. A crucial sign of the work of the Holy Spirit is forgiveness. The past is allowed to be past, and the new hope, new possibility, is allowed to emerge. "I will forgive their sins and I will no longer remember their wrongs [Jer. 31:34]."

The community of forgiveness means a redress of the power imbalance in which the genuine interdependence people have with one another is allowed to emerge free of the power structures that keep them apart (Mark 10:42–44). Thus, to "make peace" means to work to change the conditions that make for war. To "comfort" the poor means changing their situation and working to eliminate the conditions that keep them poor. The movement of the Spirit presses us to create the conditions of a Just Peace.

The Church: Peacemaking Community

God's will for the human community is that we build a Just Peace. This leads us to recognize that the making of Just Peace requires peacemakers.

Peacemakers are those who struggle to live in the presence of the Spirit; they are the friends of God.

In traditional theology, human beings have been regarded as prideful, self-seeking, and individualistic. It is assumed by Pentagon planners and many Christian theologians that because violence has saturated human history, violence is innate to the species. Only by terror, whether of hell or mutually assured destruction, can human beings be kept from destroying one another. This and other one–sidedly negative views of human nature have undercut Christians' sense of themselves as capable of moral agency.

But humanity has been decisively redefined by the advent of God in history, God's coming in Christ. Through the grace that is made present to humanity by the Holy Spirit, we are all enabled to recognize the human possibility genuinely available for constructing our world on the principles of justice.

A Just Peace church is one in which members bond together as friends of God to work as agents in history for the creation of the things that make for peace. Yet, the United Church of Christ, as well as other churches, operates with a notion of the community of the church as a collection of individuals, each of whom associates with this group because of a similarity of opinion.

That is not the community of the church. It may be that Christians cling to notions of individualism because bonding between persons is often seen in Western culture as a sign of dependence, as an admission of need, and hence as weak. On the contrary, interdependence, understood as the covenantal relation of those abiding in friendship with God, should lead us to a corporate identity capable of sustaining the difficult and divisive task of making peace, even vis-à-vis the state.

Church and State: Responsibilities for Well–being

Christians are a people bonded in covenant with God and one another as the church in order to befriend humanity in the creation of Just Peace. In addition to our church affiliation, we are members of other institutions as well. The state is one such institution.

Yet, the state is not the "world," in contrast to the "unworldliness" of the church. The church is also radically the world. We must resist any attempt to separate the church from the world or it will be hard for us to understand the world that the church and the state both share.

On the one hand, the persecution by the state of the early church and the resistance in the Reformation to the close identification of the church with the state have both left the Protestant church the legacy of a negative view of the state as an order whose sole function is to restrain evil by force.

On the other hand, when the church is too closely identified with the state, the church is seen to lose its capacity for dissent, as did the Constantinian church, which served to legitimate the status quo from the time of the early Middle Ages.

A more positive view of the state may be traced to Augustine's *City of God:* "Justice and justice alone is the only possible bond which can unite men [humanity] as a true populous in a res publica." While Augustine himself did not believe that such a state could exist in history, his vision of such an ideal state is of use today.

Differing views in the United States have combined a post–Reformation opinion of the state as an order of force with a deep faith in the religious value of this country. As a nation "with the soul of a church," as Martin Marty has said, Americans believe themselves to be established as a state on religious principles. The

Puritan legacy has been the identification of our nation with the purposes of God. So closely is this nation identified with the cause of God that any challenge to the conduct of our government is viewed by many religious persons as evil. Thus, dissent becomes not only unpatriotic but downright sinful. These views combine to subvert both a positive role for the church in regard to public issues and a prophetic role for the church in regard to dissent from public policy.

The task for a Just Peace church is to conceive a theory of the state that is positive and workable without losing the capacity of the church to dissent from the policies of the nation.

The first step in elaborating such a theory is to assert that the state is based on consent rather than coercion. The second step is to view the state as an order established to create social justice and human welfare rather than merely to restrain evil.

The state alone cannot create consensus or the ordering of human welfare without intermediate forms of cooperation and community both within the state and between states. Here Christians may begin to see a role for the church. The church, bonded in community, helps to strengthen the cooperative nature of society. But, this is not the older Constantinian notion of the church as the "cement" of the state. The Just Peace church functions to raise the level of awareness within the larger society of the need for social justice and human welfare. When the state does not make justice its first priority, the Just Peace church calls the state to task.

Responsible action for Just Peace may, therefore, also involve radical disobedience to the state when the state does not make Just Peace its priority. For example, providing sanctuary for Central American political refugees whom the U.S. government seeks to deport is a concrete and responsible act, which establishes Just Peace and points out to the state its failure to do so. Tax resistance is similarly a challenge to the state and an act of responsible obedience to Just Peace.

The church also has an important role in the relation between states for the achievement of international institutions that can promote justice. The church is not the state, and the loyalty of church members is not primarily to the state but to Christ and those to whom Christ is loyal, the human community. The church is a witness to the fact that national sovereignty is not an end in itself, and it must advocate relaxation of rabid notions of national sovereignty in order to make possible the establishment of international institutions that promote effectively the emergence of justice and peace.

Those who have viewed the primary purpose of the state as coercive (such as Reinhold Niebuhr or Paul Ramsey) have been ceaselessly frustrated because international forms of coercion do not exist. But, in fact, the coercive view of the state strengthens notions of national sovereignty and prevents any international movement from emerging.

The church, as those called to befriend humanity, has the responsibility to confront the state on issues that concern the human community. The church must also accept responsibility for the consequences to the human community of the positions it advocates.

The question has often been debated whether the church's wisdom is appropriate to government. Or, put another way, is the perspective of the gospel inherently antipolitical or apolitical and therefore inappropriate for political decision making?

One of the lessons Christians have learned from new voices in theological discourse is that the gospel is profoundly political, that it is immersed in the world, on behalf of the world. Christians are not always on the losing side, provided we understand what it means to win.

For example, one of the most profound contributions Christians have to make to the political debate on nuclear war is the Christian vision of real possibility, what we have called eschatology.

The Future: Real Hope for a Just Peace

What is the Christian hope that we will be able to construct a just and viable social order that is not based on force? Scripture points to a God known not only in the creation and as creator but also in the events of human history. This God is portrayed as having entered history as covenant partner with humankind, without reservation, in the life of Jesus of Nazareth. Thus our religious life—our life with God—is not separate from the life of the world but is indeed embodied in it. God's entrance into history has created possibilities for the world of which we can avail ourselves in a real way. Evil is not the last word on human community.

It is part of the confession to which scripture leads us that there is nothing in all creation that can separate us from the love of God in Christ Jesus (Romans 8:35f). Thus, even the horror of death in a nuclear holocaust and the search for peace into which it scares us are not a sufficient foundation for peace. Rather, it is the other pole of the continuum that pulls us toward a peace theology that is consonant with our biblical roots, namely a thirst for love and justice that takes on God's own advocacy for the poor and dispossessed. Only such a love of peace is worthy of our creation and our goal.

One of the most noticeable differences between peace theologies that have emerged from a white North

American perspective and those that have emerged from black, feminist, and Third World analyses is precisely at this juncture. What is our motivation to act to create peace?

For the black perspective to be identified legitimately in a peace theology, it must not be a theology that emerges out of fear of death and annihilation. It must not be a theology that limits violence to wars and ignores the violence present every day in the life of the poor. It must be a theology that lifts up God's will and intent in creation for a just order accessible to all. It must focus on the struggles of bringing into being a quality of life in which persons can be at peace with God, with themselves, and with others.

This black perspective is consistent with our biblical heritage as it confronts our present experience. The motivation for peace and nuclear disarmament that comes out of the fear of death is not legitimately or authentically Christian. A genuine peace theology springs from a thirst for love, justice, and equality for all people.

To base a national policy on the fear of death is to lose the vision of the state as an order based on justice. The loss of this vision has resulted in public policy that is based on apocalypticism and despair.

The church can contribute to the public policy debate over peace and the nuclear threat in many ways, but here we raise up two.

First, the church must constantly provide a prophetic critique of the state when the state fails to implement policy aimed at the fulfillment of justice. The hope for human community confronts the economies of greed. The church regards this prophetic critique as a contribution to public policy debate because the church is capable of offering an alternative view to the prevailing understanding of national security as the supreme justification of the use of any amount of force in the protection of the nation-state. On the contrary, the church offers a conception of the state as justifying its existence through the creation of justice.

Second, the church contributes a vision of human hope, without which alternatives to deterrence theory cannot emerge. The church must make clear in the public policy debate that prevailing theories of the human situation as solely one of violent aggrandizement are one-sided and distorted. Forgiveness is possible and trust can emerge. In raising human hope in the public policy debate over nuclear weapons, we in the church pose an important countervailing force in the political process. We point to the "real security" of a Just Peace society, which must replace the false security of deterrence.

5.   *REAL SECURITY*

THE INSIGHTS OF the Just Peace church are legitimately offered to the state as the state decides upon peace and justice issues. Real security is a genuine alternative to the current terror of deterrence—drawn from the vision of shalom, Just Peace.

In its purest sense, national security may be defined as safety: a nation free from the fact or threat of danger, harm, or loss. The traditional objectives of national security involve enhancing those interests perceived as vital to the preservation of the nation's peace and prosperity. National security is commonly extended to include assuring a nation of a favorable, if not advantageous, position in its relationships with other nations.

Before examining the major components of national security, three points should be made clear.

First of all, the longevity of the nation cannot be regarded alone as a measure of its security. If security is not extended to each individual, a nation, despite great age, is not free from danger, harm, or loss.

Second, achieving the conditions of security does not insure a nation against attack or economic threat. It only reinforces the probability that a nation will remain secure, while simultaneously opening the door to greater friendship with other nations.

Third, the very term "national security" is short-sighted. The security of each nation in the world is dependent on the security of all nations. In an interconnected world where the consequences of political and economic problems are increasingly felt across national boundaries, the biblical vision of Just Peace becomes an imperative. There can be no national security without global security, common security. Quite literally, the foundations of security must embrace the earth.

Real security for all relies upon four major components: provision for the defense of a nation, provision for the general well-being of a nation's citizenry, the creation of a political atmosphere and structure in which Just Peace can flourish and in which the risk of war is diminished, and the cultivation and establishment of justice. None of these components exists in a vacuum. Although each is interlocking, they will be considered individually.

Defense

A secure nation often is defined as a nation free from actual or threatened military attack and occupation. A strong military is the most tangible and symbolic dimension of that security. Following this definition, the perceived requirements of security have dictated that a nation maintain a strong defense posture capable of successfully resisting hostile or destructive actions from within or without.

While universal and complete disarmament is the ultimate goal, the realities of the modern world support the argument that a certain amount of armament is necessary to provide for a nation's defense. The problem, historically, has been the substitution of military power, and the amassing of increasingly destructive weaponry, for negotiation in the resolution of differences. Aside from the enormous economic and spiritual costs of basing security on the threat of mass destruction, excessive dependence on armament has adversely affected security aims by fueling the arms race; increasing fear, hostility and suffering; and suspending the making of real peace.

Dependence on armament reaches its peak in deterrence doctrine, which supposes that war between nations (and in particular the superpowers and their allies) may be indefinitely postponed because the risks are unacceptable. Deterrence, the operative theory behind much of the stockpiling of arms, runs counter to national security objectives for several major reasons.

Deterrence advocates assume that rival nations, restrained only by the unacceptable risks of war, stand ready to overwhelm each other at the first sign of weakness. This assumption assigns the most malevolent characteristics to the adversary nation and excludes other facts and circumstances. Thus, stockpiling in the name of deterrence results in increasing mutual fear and suspicion. National policy forged by worst-case analysis and, more importantly, by weaponry is offered as a substitute for the negotiated resolution of differences.

The Joint Chiefs of Staff *Dictionary of Military and Associated Terms* defines "national security" as the condition provided by a "military or defense advantage over any foreign nation or group of nations." But, advantages in military capabilities create anxieties and ambiguities about intentions. Whether deterrence doctrine, self-defense, or stability is at work, nations or groups that unilaterally aim to protect their interests ignore the legitimate right of others to feel secure and provoke fear and hostility.

Real security is based upon the collective security of all nations. Nations that justify their participation in the arms race as necessary to defend their national interests operate with the assumption that security can be gained at the expense of another nation. In so doing, they add fuel to the competitive drive to expand national arsenals.

Furthermore, as Herbert Scoville, Jr., a former technical director for the Department of Defense, stated, "Someday we may learn that military technology fixes are not the road to security." Indeed, Orville Wright recalled toward the end of World War I, "When my brother and I built the first [hu]man-carrying machine, we thought that we were introducing into the world an invention which would make further wars practically impossible." Short-term advantages may be cited in the production and deployment of qualitatively superior weaponry, but those who argue that this results in greater security ignore the longer-term cycle of arms and insecurity. Just as quantitative increases in weaponry lead to instabilities and fuel the arms race, so does the production and deployment of increasingly sophisticated and lethal weaponry.

The question remains, however: What constitutes an adequate defense? or How much is enough? In 1977, Secretary of Defense Harold Brown said, "I think that real security lies in strategic arms negotiations to produce a lower level of armaments and corresponding negotiations with respect to conventional arms." Brown's statement offers a clue to the answer: fewer weapons and a reversal of threatening military postures. Parity is seen by some to be the aim of arms reductions (or arms acquisitions). The real aim of defense security policies must be to make all sides more secure at the lowest possible level of armament, with the end goal of abolishing all weapons and the need for them. Only those kinds of policies will allow present and future generations to live without threat of a return to the violence of war.

Well-being

Hosea told the people of ancient Israel, "Because you have trusted in your chariots and in the multitudes of your warriors, therefore the tumult of war shall rise among your people and all your fortresses shall be destroyed [Hos. 10:13–14]." Dwight D. Eisenhower echoed those words before he assumed office as the thirty-fourth President of the United States: "The problem with defense is how far you can go without destroying from within what you are trying to defend from without."

Aside from the provocative nature of excessive arms expenditures, a national security policy based on such expenditures can increase nonmilitary threats to security. These threats include chronic inflation and unemployment, diversion of investment funds from the civilian economy, deterioration of the public infrastructure, retardation of civilian technological progress, competition for funds for domestic and foreign aid and development programs, and citizen frustration. Each of these stresses is a force with which the military cannot (and is not designed to) cope. The exacerbating effect of heavy arms spending is already evident in the U.S. economy and has been well documented by experts in economics and history. While military expenditures have some limited, short-term economic benefits, overall they contribute to economic and social hardship. This in turn creates new dangers and instabilities that erode national and global security.

When poverty, disease, hunger, violence, and political repression exist in any nation, their consequences are felt in and among all nations. People who lack the basic necessities of life, and whose ability to shape a secure future is shackled, provide the seeds for social unrest and the erosion of social cohesion, thereby threatening the safety of all individuals and nations. Historically, oppressed and exploited people do not remain passive forever.

The drive to secure superior standards of living by exploiting others and their resources often takes the form of "economic colonialism" (neocolonialism). Individuals, nations, and corporations that seek to gain social and economic advantages over others aggravate social hardship and economic ills. As Julius Nyerere, Tanzanian president, said, "Our national economies are linked: the poverty or prosperity of one country affects the economy of all others. When potential customers are too poor to buy, the manufacturer suffers—internationally as well as nationally." In an economically interdependent world, there is no longer a national economy; there are only branches of a global economy.

The economic and social well-being of people within individual nations necessitates the collective well-being of all people in all nations. Real security requires that basic human needs are met and that people are not threatened with poverty and deprivation. The objective of national economic policies should be consistent with the collective welfare of all people, with the fundamental goal of reducing inequities, sharing benefits, and providing an enhanced quality of life and dignity for all. Such policies will require a deep restructuring of present international economic relations and a reorientation of development and aid

74

strategies toward meeting basic human needs and guaranteeing human rights to people everywhere in the world.

Political Structure

Coincident with defense and economic security objectives is the establishment of a climate of cooperation, peace, and hope for a secure future. Patronage, belligerence, and exploitation cause (or create) fear, which in turn breeds suspicion, hatred, and revenge. These complexes press toward violence and erode the security of nations and individuals. An atmosphere of trust and understanding involves constructive and curative actions so that violent confrontations in the resolution of conflicts of interest can be preempted. In expressing national policies, the rights of others must be respected, lest the security of all be diminished.

Security is often sought through the accumulation and exercise of power conceived as strength. The task of governments and individuals who seek lasting and real security is to design ways of sharing power and keeping power exposed to criticism and limiting it without producing continual stalemates. Such arrangements of power enhance all varieties of security and provide a political climate in which the risk of war is diminished because conflict can be managed and resolved nonviolently.

That nations go to war is also a reflection of the weakness of an international system that has an inadequate structure of laws acceptable and observed by all nations and groups. Whether it is national, regional, or global, a centralized authority vested with the power to govern its members is a basic requirement for meeting security needs. Such an authority, if it is to survive and serve the needs of those governed, must be an elastic and impartial structure that can equitably and nonviolently resolve disputes between nations and groups as time and circumstances require. A prerequisite of such a structure is the ability of its members to make demands effectively. This ability requires the structural embodiment of the fundamental human rights of self-determination and individual political participation, through which the achievement of social and economic rights becomes possible. The fundamental values of such a structure must be openness, responsiveness, sharing, cooperation, and the pursuit and administration of justice.

Justice

Justice is a fundamental source of real security, and without it, there can be no real security, no lasting peace. Wrongs and inequities—whether systemic, corporate, or personal—generate tension and conflict, which historically have led to the erosion or outright destruction of security. Justice dictates that all actions and judgments be impartial, righteous, and equitable. Justice requires that, in the words of the Interreligious Task Force on U.S. Food Policy, "human dignity is recognized, human rights are respected, and human needs fulfilled." Such actions form the basis for a transforming justice that reinforces the security of all.

Justice demands an equitable sharing of, and access to, human and material resources. The sharing and access must span time as well as distance, because the consequences of actions good and bad, right and wrong, spread both across our lives and through the ages.

76

Justice must reach not only across and around our globe but deep into the future.

Those seeking security are challenged to cultivate, establish, and administer an uncompromising and transforming justice. Only then will lasting safety and real security be firmly grounded.

The building of real national and global security is no simple task. Strategists must recognize and grasp the dynamic forces within society that make for security and insecurity. Policies, actions, and cooperative efforts must reflect the complex relationships of critical elements of security.

The work of building security for all will take time, attention, and thought. It will require insight, compassion, and understanding. These attributes are not easily applied in a complex and chaotic world. But, as President Kenneth Kaunda of Zambia, has said:

> All the political goodwill and all the instruments of social and economic development at the disposal of the rich and poor countries must be combined and harnessed with a new spirit of dedication, sacrifice, wisdom, and foresight to meet our common obligation to the whole of humanity. . . . The challenge is not just simply the elimination of poverty, ignorance, and disease. It is first and foremost a question of building a world in which every man, woman, and child, without distinction, will have and exercise the right to live a full human life worthy of his or her person, free from servitude, oppression, and exploitation imposed on him or her by other fellow human beings; a world in which freedom, peace, and security will have practical meaning to each and every member of the human race.*

---

*From an address to the Food and Agricultural Organization of the World Conference on Agrarian Reform and World Development, Rome, Italy, 1979.

Common security is the presence of Just Peace, God's intention for human community. It is within the capability of humankind. Despite miscarried efforts throughout all of history, the vision remains and can be glimpsed here and there. It is the responsibility of the Just Peace church to hold up this vision as clearly and as concretely as possible.

6.

THE JUST PEACE CHURCH: LIVING IN THE PRESENCE OF THE SPIRIT

IN FACING UP to the weighty questions of public policy, the church is also confronting a crisis in its own faith life. The questions now raised for us are these: Can the church really be the faithful Body of Christ in its mission and ministry in the world? Can it proclaim the good news of God's mission of justice and peace for the world and verify its faith through witnessing to the truths it proclaims? Or must the church succumb to the pressures of maintaining its financial security and perhaps even its structural integrity at the cost of its faithfulness to the gospel?

It is possible that being faithful to the gospel may cause the church to lose the support of those structures and institutions that aid it in its mission and ministry. The church's faithfulness to the vision of Just Peace also may cause it to lose the commitment of those members of the Body of Christ who are still filled with fears, anxieties, and mistrust about definitions of, and avenues to, security and cannot bring themselves to trust in what they perceive to be the unreassuring precariousness of the real security found in God.

Yet, if the church is less than faithful to the gospel, it undermines its own foundations. And, if the church is insufficiently critical of the world and the deceptive idols of security-based blind nationalism, military strength, technological solutions to human problems, self-centered materialism, and stability without regard for justice, it risks losing those portions of its own body that support and are committed to striving for a Just Peace.

Though the risks are great, the church must not fail to enter into God's history of creating a Just Peace. The neutrality of the church is an illusion: either the church takes a prophetically critical position in favor of the peace and ultimate security found in God, or it silently supports those idolatrous structures that act against both the future and the restoration of human community.

Historically and traditionally, the United Church of Christ has operated on the premise that congregations are autonomous corporate bodies that can and do act independently of the wider church. While freedom and diversity are to be upheld, the covenantal relationship among local congregations, associations, conferences, and the wider church needs to be examined. However widely dismissed, it is a cherished ideal of many people that the wider church is so united and uniting that it can speak to and for all people, but the choice between a "traditional" church and a prophetic church calls into question this ideal. The Just Peace church, as a prophetic church, must speak out boldly and clearly on issues of justice and peace. The covenantal relationships that bind its parts together must give it the needed strength of a corporate identity capable of sustaining the difficult and often divisive task of building a Just Peace.

But what is a Just Peace church? What does it do? The answers are many. The Just Peace church is a covenantal community that recognizes its calling and accepts the risk of being faithful. It seeks reconciliation within the world and builds human community despite the determination of some to remain divided. It affirms peace with justice. It affirms the rich diversity of patterns of political and economic relationships that reflect a shared vision of the intended wholeness of God's creation. It offers hope to all and nurtures those who lack the discipline of trust in God's promise of peace and justice.

In order to realize more fully both our capacity and our calling to be agents and advocates of Just Peace in the world, the United Church of Christ, as a Just Peace church, will need to reexamine itself and its structure. Where necessary, it will need to reorient itself so as to make the greatest impact on the issues of justice, injustice, peace, and violence.

This section deals with the life of the Just Peace church. It offers reflections on the marks of a Just Peace church as well as practical suggestions and ideas for worship, education, organizing, and outreach for individuals and faith communities. These reflections are a beginning point for us as a community of faithful witnesses to explore individually and corporately how we might more fully be incarnations of God's intentional, covenantal, reckless, and excessive love.

Marks of a Just Peace Church

The Just Peace church is a church that organizes itself and functions for God's radical mission of justice and peace to the world. Its being is proclaimed and lived by the "gospel of peace," which it shares with the world (Ephesians 6:15; Romans 10:15; Isaiah 52:7). Its life under the rule of Christ is marked by a continual searching for "the things that make for peace [Luke 19:42; Rom. 14:19]."

The Just Peace church proclaims God's promise of peace and justice for all and works to fulfill that promise. The Just Peace church, in proclaiming and doing, is continually growing in faith in Jesus Christ and understanding of the centrality of peacemaking to the gospel. It works unceasingly to expand the vision of a Just Peace and seeks to discover new and creative ways to build Just Peace. The Just Peace church equips its members for God's mission and exemplifies in its own life the peace that God gives to the world.

In so doing, in an age when despair and doubt about the possibility of Just Peace in our time fill the hearts and minds of many, the Just Peace church must nurture hope. The Just Peace church cannot be a community of faith without proclaiming the liberating message of hope and trust to the fearful and faithless. Hope affirms the promise that peace will be triumphant—that there will be a Just Peace for ourselves, for our children, and for our children's children. Hope gives us the strength of mind and voice so that we can come to a world not merely of our own making but of our own choosing.

As members of the United Church of Christ, we proclaim "grace and peace from God." Now we all must earnestly seek to give witness to what this means as a Just Peace church in the world where injustice and violence oppress millions. As members of the Body of Christ, who though many are one and who possess differing gifts but the same Spirit, we are a people who seek completeness and unity for ourselves and the world. "Christ is our peace," the letter to the Ephesians reminds us, "who has made us both one, and has broken down the dividing wall of hostility [Eph. 2:14]."

We recognize, though, that "we have this treasure in earthen vessels [2 Cor. 4:7]." Throughout our lives and our world, the peace of Christ is fragile and often broken. The "dividing walls of hostility" continue to be rebuilt, over and over again. While we proclaim ourselves to be people of faith, we recognize that "faith is the assurance of things hoped for, the conviction of things not seen [Heb. 11:1]." We recognize our commonness with our mothers and fathers in the faith, with Sarah and Abraham, with Moses and Zipporah, who "all died in faith, not having received what was promised, but having seen it and greeted it from afar, and having acknowledged that they were strangers and exiles on the earth [Heb. 11:13]." Like them, we "desire a better country, that is, a heavenly one [Heb. 11:16]," but we realize it is not here yet.

We know that we live in a broken world where "wounds have been healed lightly" and people cry, "Peace, peace, where there is no peace [Jer. 6:14]." Despite our visions and hopes for universal shalom, the lion and the lamb have not lain down together. Yet the vision and promise of God is that the lion and the lamb shall lie down together in harmony. The vision is *not* the lion driven out from the land or killed, leaving the lamb to feed undisturbed. Such a picture, frequently encountered in our history, leads us to confess that our yearning for peace is as yet unfulfilled.

Neither does the world now live with the reality of everyone living unafraid under his or her vine and fig tree (Mic. 4:4). The economic well-being envisioned by the Old Testament prophet, Micah, was a hallmark of shalom. Today, far too many of us have greedily reaped and raped fig tree and vineyard, leaving others to suffer abject poverty and death. The material deprivation of the world's dispossessed is evidence, once again, that God's reign is incomplete.

The absence of the complete reign of God in the world today does not give us the right to excuse our complicity in its incompleteness. In our faith life and in our worship, we need to begin to see the lion and the lamb living together, not as the fruit of war but as the gift of grace. We also need to see the poor and oppressed of the world as victims of oppression and exploitation, not as targets outside the church who deserve a helping hand or as the "price" of a capitalist economy. We must identify ourselves as brother and sister of both lamb and lion, for Christ "is our peace, who has made us both one [Eph. 2:14]." The vision awaits us. Our mission is to bind the broken reality of our world into the wholeness of the universal healing gospel of Jesus Christ and to incorporate ourselves into God's mission of justice and rightness, building communities of faithful and celebrating servants, conscious of our solidarity with brothers and sisters the world over.

The tasks of ministry of the Just Peace church are to discover, receive, celebrate, and share in God's mission of justice and righteousness. As such, the Just Peace church examines in our social location the biblical and theological basis for a Just Peace. It develops and equips people with the skills for engaging in the saving work of God in Jesus Christ. The Just Peace church creates the peacemaking community at local, regional, and international levels; and it supports the witness of its members as they actively seek to bring forth the fulfillment of creation. It enriches this witness in mutual nurturing of the vision and creation of the strategies for action.

In worship, the Just Peace church celebrates its justice and peacemaking identity. Its worship draws attention to what God is doing in its midst and who it is as the community of faith. In its worship it empowers the people to be agents and advocates of a Just Peace.

As agent and advocate of Just Peace, the Just Peace church reaches out across all boundaries, meeting and establishing dialogue with those perceived as enemy,

creating new realities of global community. The Just
Peace church does not ignore or deny the harsh realities
of government and people who withhold dignity and
life from the world. Instead, it works with unleashed
adventure and creativity to thwart destructive myths
and memories and to build new realities.

As agent and advocate of Just Peace, the Just Peace
church stands with the oppressed, creating community
and solidarity with the dispossessed and the victims of
unjust structures. In standing with them, the Just Peace
church does not set the poor over the rich or the
oppressed over the oppressor. It affirms that all come
under God's love and care. In recognizing God's
unmistakable identification with the poor and
oppressed, the Just Peace church works through, with,
and for the dispossessed to gain freedom from those
who destroy life, justice, and mercy.

As agent and advocate of Just Peace, the Just Peace
church recognizes and assumes its own complicity in
the responsibility for national and global order. It also
assumes responsibility for changing national and global
order. The Just Peace church does not isolate itself from
the international human community, nor does it
assume that there is one kind of order that should be
applied to all nations. Rather, the Just Peace church
seeks to discover and sustain varieties of order that
emphasize justice and mutual interdependence and
that effectively resolve conflict without the use of
violence.

A Just Peace and Our Faith Life

In 1981, the delegates to General Synod XIII
declared that peace would be one of the priorities of the
United Church of Christ for a four-year period. While

special emphasis is certainly warranted, peace is more than simply an issue or a programmatic emphasis in which the church and its members become involved when circumstances or events call for a response. Peace is never extraneous or peripheral to the gospel but is an integral part of it, indivisible from our faith life. Through God in Christ we receive the gift of grace experienced as peace.

In joyful recognition and receipt of God's gift of shalom in our lives, we celebrate and share the good news of God's peace. Our response to this gift cannot be to retreat from the world and its illness into the sanctuary of our own private lives and congregations. It is an insufficient response to feel that being a faithful Christian simply means becoming a useful member of a congregation, serving on its committees, worshiping with friends, and accomplishing narrowly defined evangelism tasks of teaching about, and seeking conversion of others to, Christ. The fullness of God's mission in the world demands that we heed the call to enter the world as lovers who wish to serve it and redeem it. As Paul tells the Ephesians, "This may be a wicked age, but your lives should redeem it [Eph. 5:16]."

As the Body of Christ, the community of believers has become the temple—the place where God makes peace between the divine and the human and between humans. Paul, in his letter to the Corinthians, refers to people as God's temple: "Do you not know that you are God's temple and that God's Spirit dwells in you? If any one destroys God's temple, God will destroy him [or her]. For God's temple is holy, and that temple you are [1 Cor. 3:16–17]." In the same epistle, the point is made from a slightly different angle: "Do you not know that your body is a temple of the Holy Spirit within you, which you have from God [1 Cor. 6:19]?" Our body as

86

the temple of the Holy Spirit—as the justice advocate through which Jesus Christ is made present to the Christian community—means that God makes the church body, the community of believers, a peacemaker. So, then, is each individual body; it can be especially said of the church: "Blessed are the peacemakers [Matt. 5:9]."

The temple—the faithful community of believers— does not seek to escape the brokenness of the world but enters into the life-and-death struggle for the redemption of the world. It joins with God to love, care for, celebrate, and suffer with people as justice and righteousness are built. In saying, "You are the salt *of the earth*. . . . You are the light *of the world* [Matt. 5:13–14: italics added]," Jesus has called us to involved action here and now *in the world*, to be seekers and makers of a Just Peace in the world we live in today.

Baptism is a primary sign of our liberation to be agents and advocates of a Just Peace. The eucharist is a second sign.

In baptism, we are liberated into life; we receive a new identity as individual persons and are implanted into the temple community where we become agents and advocates of Just Peace and members of the Body of Jesus Christ, who brought the new peace. Baptism witnesses to the reality of Ephesians 2:14: "For Christ is our peace, who has made us both one, and has broken down the dividing wall of hostility." It sets us in cooperative solidarity with the people of God, the Body of Christ, and our suffering solidarity with all oppressed people is signified by the cross. In baptism, we become marked with the life-giving waters of God, marked with a symbol and words that call us to bring Just Peace into the world.

In receiving the eucharistic meal, we are also liberated; we receive a new identity as community. As

Christ is re-membered among us, we receive in community both the justice meal and a vision, rooted in hope, of what God intends for all: we are provided for and receive forgiveness from God. In receiving Holy Communion, we are nourished by the love of Christ and are called into communion with all people. The model Christ gives us includes an element that many have difficulty accepting: as forgiveness and provision are offered, they are offered in community even to the one who would betray Jesus. In our own Holy Meals, though betrayal is not the mark, separation and enmity can be, yet the bread and cup of reconciliation and restoration is available to all.

Our new identity is offered to us again and again in the eucharist. We are constituted ever anew as the body of peacemakers who offer the world an alternative way of life: the way of Just Peace. What we especially celebrate in the eucharist is the peace that passes all understanding, which becomes effective in our struggle for a Just Peace in the world.

Our new identity as makers of Just Peace is immersed in the Holy Spirit, the power of the gospel word to break down dividing walls and restore the world to wholeness. Our new identity is drenched in the new wine of the Spirit, and just as old wineskins cannot hold new wine, so we do not have the capacity to maintain an old status quo where God's peace and God's justice are unfulfilled. We restlessly bear the Spirit's peace in a world not yet at peace. The Holy Spirit provides the church, individually and corporately, with life-giving new wineskins bubbling with the ferment of justice, peace, and the upbuilding of community. The Spirit creates our new identity—our new humanity— and is thus the content of both baptism and Holy Communion.

At the center of our life of faith, as the individual and corporate Body of Christ immersed in our identity as makers of Just Peace living in the presence of the Spirit, is the building of a Just Peace. The challenge is to discover how to do that. The following pages offer specific suggestions for integrating the making of peace and justice into worship, education, and outreach programs of individual congregations so that they permeate our life of faith.

A Just Peace and Worship

In worship, the Just Peace church celebrates the work of God in the midst of conflict and injustice and calls us to become part of the work of God's giving of Just Peace. The worshiping community of the Just Peace church reflects the centrality of Just Peace to its life of faith and manifests this concern not only through the content of its liturgy but also through the relationships and value systems enacted there.

The Just Peace church affirms the oneness of all people, in common need of the receipt of God's grace experienced as peace. In worship, the community of believers is challenged, strengthened, and empowered to join in God's justice and peace giving; worship sustains the community with visions and hopes that advocate life and celebrate with thanksgiving God's presence throughout the world. Worship and peacemaking are inseparably bound to each other. Neither is superimposed upon the other.

Because worship is not limited to a time on Sunday morning or a room called the sanctuary but draws together all that we have and are and do, it raises the questions, Whom do we love most? Where is our security ultimately rooted? Because these issues are raised in all parts of our lives, our whole lives are the content of our worship.

Through worship, people can be sustained in the long journey toward creation of Just Peace. The huge task of creating a Just Peace can create in some a sense of being too small, too tired, too unwise, too powerless to redeem themselves or the world. Some people feel overwhelmed by the demands on time and self, the risk and complexity of the task, the suffering required and the suffering observed. The abundance of fear and the divisiveness of being makers of peace and justice nurture the temptation to withdraw from, ignore, or thwart the process of seeking and building a Just Peace. The central theme of all worship, and especially in times when the making of peace and justice is brought into sharpened focus, is to nurture and celebrate hope, while empowering people to *be* builders of Just Peace. Hope gives people the strength of heart and voice to change the world, to choose life, even when margins for success seem slim.

Worship is also an occasion when people's spiritual lives can be deepened and strengthened. Through prayer and other reflective acts such as fasting and silence, people lift up their consciousness of God's presence in history and self and are infused with the spirit and will to be agents and advocates of God's mission of love, justice, and mercy in the world. Through both personal and corporate worship, hope is nurtured and we are released from our captivity to forces that oppose God's liberating mission of redemption.

There are many ways to incorporate Just Peace into congregational worship. In some churches, the issue is not *how* but *whether* Just Peace will be made central to their worship life. Controversy is likely to erupt when Just Peace is preached about, prayed for, sung of, read about, or acted on. For many church leaders, this challenge to confront injustice and violence leads to potentially destructive disagreement within the congregation. It is important to be sensitive to the receptiveness of the congregation and select the most effective means of communication. When tensions arise, they can be used as an opportunity to demonstrate ways to promote reconciliation.

The clergy play an especially critical role in making Just Peace central to the entire life of the congregation. Their leadership in building a Just Peace is often the igniting force that helps empower a congregation to be agent and advocate of Just Peace in both personal and political dimensions.

In those congregations where Just Peace concerns are not part of the corporate worship life, individuals and groups can approach the clergy or worship committee and ask that such concerns be included. It may be helpful to offer suggestions and assistance. Persistence may be required, as well as the support and expressed concern of other individuals and groups within the congregation.

Just Peace can be incorporated into worship services in a variety of ways. The following are illustrative.

Suggestions for Incorporating Just Peace Concerns into Worship

- Use symbols as ways of creatively opening up Just Peace issues. Use one or more candles as symbols of hope for peace, as reminders of our need for Just Peace and our commitment to it. Focus on bread and cup as symbols of God's reconciling and merciful love. Use different ways to "pass the peace." Use, for example, balloons, flowers, seeds, children's toys, canned goods, toy brick walls, to heighten awareness of Just Peace concerns and open up new dimensions of reality.

- Pray! Invite people to write on slips of paper during the prelude: "Places where peace is needed . . . " or "Today, I yearn for peace in . . . " Collect the slips and let the worship leader or pastor state the petitions during morning prayers.

- Let the pastoral prayer include petitions drawn from the newspaper regarding places where people are fighting or dying. Be specific! Or pray specifically for our legislators as they consider issues, bills, budgets, and other matters so that their decisions may bring peace.

- Try using a meditative style of prayer. Guide the people with words, pausing after each sentence. Encourage them to envision events or situations and the way transformations and reconciliations can occur. Have them feel the breath of God's presence fill the event or situation they are envisioning, feeling the wind of God's Spirit blowing over them and empowering them as well as those they envision. After a pause at the end of a guided prayer meditation, the organ or piano might lead into a response: "Hear our prayer, O Lord."*

- *Read the scriptures!* Invite the congregation to move up to the edge of their chairs, lean forward, perk up their ears—and *hear* the Word of God. Repeat words and phrases in passages so that they can sink into speaker and hearer alike, emphasizing different words each time the phrase is repeated, as in, "Blessed— Blessed—Blessed are the peacemakers!— Peacemakers! For they shall be called the children of God—the *children* of God—the children of *God.*"

---

*The Hymnal, No. 501. New York: United Church Press.

Invite the congregation to repeat various parts of a
passage or an entire passage—and have it read in
short, appropriate phrases.

- Read the same passage from several different versions
  of the Bible, such as the Revised Standard Version,
  King James Version, Good News, Jerusalem, Cotton
  Patch, and the Inclusive Language Lectionary. Let
  people hear the nuances and special meaning
  reflected in them. Read the scriptures in Spanish or in
  the languages of other nations where there is
  oppression and strife to stress that *God* is speaking
  these languages to us today.
- Use nonscriptural reading to supplement scriptural
  readings. Personal witness accounts, poems,
  newspaper headlines, and stories can all be
  incorporated into a worship service to enlighten,
  provoke, inspire, or unify people.
- Preach the Word: that's a real source of power for
  building a Just Peace! Base words on the call from a
  peacemaker, Christ, to us to be peacemakers. And
  preach, sharing uncertainties and fears, as well as
  "truths." Let sermons invite people to join the search
  and struggle for a Just Peace. Show how Just Peace is
  an integral part of the life of faith. Challenge people to
  action and involvement in light of their faith, and
  point out the relation between faith and politics. Be
  accurate in reporting current events and analyses, and
  relate these to faith issues.
- Invite commitment and action during worship.
  Receive an offering of letters: invite people to write
  letters on general issues of peace and justice or on
  specific legislative bills before Congress. Have them
  bring the letters to the altar to be dedicated or invite
  people to write during the prelude. Let the dedication
  prayer invite God's blessing on these efforts for a Just
  Peace. Invite people to sign a faith pledge that focuses

on a stance toward the world or taking a specific action. Each time Holy Communion is received, have people bring in canned goods for the hungry as an act of thanksgiving for the nourishment received at the Table and as an act of solidarity in hope with brothers and sisters who are physically undernourished.

- Give people an opportunity to share their concerns about justice and peace, both personal and political, during worship. During announcement and concerns times, allow people to share joys, pains, and calls to action. The congregation can undergird the efforts of individuals through hearing and responding to calls for action, events, and experiences of others. When people are allowed to share their concerns openly, the work of peacemaking has begun.

- Involve groups of people in planning worship. Together they can explore the lectionary passages with the worship leaders and bring new insights to the Word. Group planning such as this reinforces the shared nature of all ministry, helps build community, and involves people in a new way of discovering the gospel. The group can help decide how to communicate the message of the passages selected.

- Look at the calendar. Note events in the past or designated observance days and seasons in the present that suggest themes of Just Peace. Offer worship services on those days or during the week that reflect on the themes of peace, justice, and freedom.

- Use inclusive language, which can expand our imagery of God and people and lessen the struggle for our children in the future. At the very least, scripture readings require some individual effort so that language describing persons becomes inclusive, as for example, brothers *and sisters*, children or partners of God (not just "sons"), humanity. Language related to

God may present a difficult problem for some, but the goals should be to expand our understanding rather than narrow it and to maintain the message of the passage. Hymns can also be revised to incorporate inclusive language, as well as language that is less warlike. Resources are available that contain revised hymns, as well as new songs (e.g., *Everflowing Streams*, ed. Ruth C. Duck and Michael G. Bausch [New York: Pilgrim Press, 1981]; *Because We Are One People*, Ecumenical Women's Center [1653 W. School St., Chicago, IL 60657]; *The Inclusive Language Lectionary* [Philadelphia/New York: Westminster Press/Pilgrim Press, 1983–1985]).

- Lift up themes of solidarity with brothers and sisters around the world. Work at building a sense of global community. Use songs and stories from other lands. When there is a eucharist, use breads native to other nations and cultures. Find prayers and litanies from other lands and cultures that can be used in the liturgy.
- Invite people in the congregation to write songs of peace and justice or put new words to old tunes. Short, simple phrases can be sung, for example, to the tune of "Slow Alleluia."
- Incorporate drama and/or dance into worship services. Have children or adults (or both) mime or do a liturgical dance of scripture passages or the Lord's Prayer or of other readings such as the World Peace Prayer: "Lead me from death to life, from falsehood to truth. Lead me from despair to hope, from fear to trust. Lead me from hate to love, from war to peace. Let peace fill our hearts, our world, our universe. Amen."

These are but a few suggestions for incorporating Just Peace into worship; there are many more, and they are limited only by the creative imagination of those involved in planning and leading worship. In searching for ways to bring Just Peace alive in worship, people may feel the need to use novel approaches. While new liturgical forms can bring new insights and excitement into worship, ancient and simple forms can and should be used: litanies that enlist congregational participation, the passing of the peace that symbolizes our reconciliation, public prayers and assurances of pardon that confess the reality of brokenness in our midst, benedictions that remind us we carry God's peace with us out into the world. Reclaimed and reinterpreted, these ancient liturgical forms can be just as vital as new forms; they have been preserved because our forebears found in them the means of amazing grace.

A Just Peace and Education

Studying peace and justice issues is an essential part of building Just Peace. Through study, the Just Peace church can begin to discover how God is acting in our midst and what is the biblical and theological basis for the church's involvement. It can also delve into complex issues and struggle to understand what is involved, what is at stake, and what the church's role should be. Study can also help us to see the world through new lenses, to get outside of our own isolated histories and experiences. Insights and knowlege will give the Just Peace church and its members a basis for decision making.

In transforming social movements, there are generally three phases: (1) consciousness raising, (2) consensus building, and (3) mobilizing. In the first phase, awareness and understanding of issues is increased. Through experiences, stories, and study, insights and knowledge are gained. In the second phase, people work together to reach a mutual understanding of and appreciation for an issue, reconcile differences, and determine a common course of action. The third and final phase is that of action: people work together to achieve a common goal. The phases overlap, with various people at different stages of understanding, agreement, and commitment. It is important to recognize that if a group bypasses or does not complete the first two phases, the ultimate actions taken are often ineffective or inappropriate. Seemingly allied groups dissolve into competing factions or founder in confusion, apathy, or mistrust. As such, consciousness raising—study and education—play a critical role in initiating and sustaining Just Peace efforts.

Educational efforts should not be limited to study groups, discussions, program series, weekend retreats, or convocations. Efforts can include leaflets and flyers, games, story telling, dramatizations, art projects, worship experiences, displays and media work, as well as the action dimensions of Just Peace such as hunger walks and food drives, visits to members of Congress, and social service in the community.

Neither should educational efforts regarding Just Peace focus entirely on international issues. Community issues such as job training and youth unemployment, fair housing, prison ministries, family violence, and female athletic budgets are all Just Peace issues that need to be addressed. In addition, personal peace issues are topics of concern. People who are distressed over problems in family communication or broken relationships, or who are filled with despair over community and global events are in need of peace ministry. All of these are concerns where people committed to a Just Peace are called into service.

Be prepared for disagreement over methods, actions, even fundamental approaches to seeking peace. Honor the diversity of views. In fact, if such conflict does not arise, encourage it! If people do not have differing points of view, then the level of discussion is too superficial. Remember: it is not conflict that is evil, but violence. When conflict is suppressed, there is false peace. One task for peacemaking is to bring conflict to the surface and work through it in community. Work toward building the kind of community in which even people who seriously disagree with one another can embrace in love. Despite the difficulty of dealing with controversy, encouraging it to erupt where it exists can enable and empower people to share freely their thoughts, fears, and uncertainties. Thus, undercurrents of powerlessness and fear do not later impede progress toward building a Just Peace.

Suggestions for Integrating Just Peace Concerns and Education

The following is a list of some of the ways Just Peace education efforts can begin.

- The Bible is one of the richest resources in peace studies. Jesus and the prophets all have much to say about conflict, justice, peace, power, and politics. Jesus, the supreme peacemaker, offers a model for loving others and celebrating life. Hence, biblical study is both vital and empowering to gain theological understandings of Just Peace efforts.
- Establish a North American version of the Latin American *comunidades de base* ("base communities"). In Latin America, these groups meet regularly to worship, pray, study the Word, and act on it. Their life has had a major influence on the church

of Latin America, as well as on Latin American society. Base communities give people a forum for building community, for discovering the Word, for empowering people, and for practicing peacemaking and enacting the Word in the world. Ernesto Cardenal's four-volume series, *The Gospel in the Solentiname*, provides an example of how base communities have worked in Nicaragua. Base community experiences help individuals and groups to examine the points of oppression within their own lives, as well as the lives of others, such that Just Peace work can begin.

• Integrate Just Peace studies into all educational programs of the congregation, such as confirmation classes, Sunday school classes, and membership instructional programs. Do not leave Just Peace concerns only to adults, either. Young children's and youth's educational programs, both in terms of content and leadership style, are a forum for beginning peace education at an early age.

• Help bring speakers into the congregation or community. Local peace and justice groups, as well as universities and colleges, can often arrange for speakers. Publicize events that are held, both within the congregation and the wider community. Plan ecumenical events that draw together people of different faiths and practices. Engage people in a dialogue on differing faith perspectives and denominational stances.

• Plan a retreat on Just Peace. A storehouse of resource and curriculum material is available for such a retreat. Planners need to determine what aspects of Just Peace they want to focus on and then figure out how to illuminate them.

• Design and distribute a "Just Peace" calendar. Research facts and figures to include in the calendar, as well as significant historical events. Include art work by members of the congregation, and use quotations from scriptural and other sources that express an empowering celebration and vision of life. Include events within the congregation and community on the calendar—meetings, school activities, worship times, cultural and national holidays, for example—as a way of laying the life of the church and the world alongside each other. Be sure to include national holidays of other lands, reinforcing the global nature of mission and ministry.

- Ask the Christian education committee to arrange church school sessions that focus on Just Peace. The UCC curriculum, *Peace Futuring*, as well as other resources, is available through the Office for Church in Society (105 Madison Avenue, New York, NY 10016). Other denominations also have a variety of peace and justice studies available for people of all ages.
- Join national coalitions and networks that advocate Just Peace, such as IMPACT (110 Maryland Avenue, N.E., Washington, DC 20002), The Coalition for a New Foreign and Military Policy (712 G Street, S.E., Washington, DC 20003), and the Parenting for Peace and Justice Network (4144 Lindell Boulevard, St. Louis, MO 63108). Each offers a variety of resources applicable to various groups, as well as analyses of a variety of issues.
- Train church leaders within the congregation in conflict management. The UCC Office for Church Life and Leadership can offer suggestions for resource material, as well as ideas on how conflict management training events might be conducted. Invite "observers" to attend church council or consistory meetings. Have them report back what they observed in terms of group dynamics and conflict management. Learn new

ways to handle conflict through creative
communication, decision making, and problem
solving so that trust is built and power is balanced. An
excellent resource book is *Church Fights: Managing
Conflict in the Local Church* by Speed Leas and Paul
Kittlaus (Philadelphia: Westminster Press, 1973).
• Gather peace literature and flyers and set up a display
in the church or at religious events or local fairs. Invite
people to take or purchase the material.
• Suggest resources and books to the Christian
education committee or the public library and ask that
they be made available.
• Encourage the showing of audiovisual material.
Schedule the showing of contemporary audiovisuals
that deal with issues the congregation is concerned
about—and look for ones that might encourage the
congregation to deal with issues it has ignored or
avoided.
• Gather people together for an afternoon or evening
simulation game that raises issues about security and
the dynamics of power, such as "Power Play"
(included in the UCC *Peace Futuring* curriculum).
Allow plenty of time to "debrief" the game—to share
insights gained from the simulation experience.
• Feature peacemaking skits and music performed by
youth and other age groups, at a dinner or program.
Invite people to rewrite and act out the parables in a
modern-day setting.
• Invite children and youth to make a mural based on
Francis of Assissi's prayer for peace ("Lord, make me
an instrument of thy peace"). Post the mural in a place
in the church building where it will be visible to the
whole congregation.
• Arrange panel discussions that present opposing
views on social issues. Allow time for discussions after
presentations have been made. Examine the moral,

spiritual, and theological issues involved and how these are applied (or ignored) by participants. Try not to create situations where adversarial rhetoric or angry debates polarize people and eliminate the possibility of genuine dialogue and bridge building. Work toward achieving a mutual understanding of the issues.

- Approach different groups within the congregation or community; share your concerns about Just Peace and ask that they make it one of their priorities. Suggest ways that these concerns can be incorporated into the life and work of the group, especially as they relate to the goals of the group.
- Sponsor people to serve as interns in the various Instrumentalities of the United Church of Christ, especially the Office for Church in Society. Or sponsor individuals on overseas mission programs. Have them return to share their learnings with others.
- Be patient. Peace education is continuous; new life and insights and truths spring forth from study. While the results of educational efforts may not be evident immediately, the efforts are never made in vain.

Just Peace and Outreach

The beatitude "Blessed are the peacemakers [Matt. 5:9]" calls for action: peacemakers are blessed—those who practice active and aggressive love. In seeking peace and building it, the Body of Christ becomes part of the good news of God's saving work.

Action and outreach involve two essential tasks: mobilizing the public will and helping to shape public policy. Public opinion, public acts of witnessing, and ultimately, political decisions will be the fulcrum upon which the fate of the world will be determined. In mobilizing the public will for Just Peace, the public is informed about issues, concerns are shared, community is built, and visions are upheld. In shaping public policy, the public will is translated into governmental administrative policies and legislation that help secure a Just Peace. Shaping public policy involves analyzing policy proposals, lobbying political decision makers, mobilizing broad-based grass-roots support, and communicating religious views through the public communications media. Both tasks involve different purposes and often demand different skills and actions. Because of the size of the task of mobilizing the public will and shaping public policy, effective efforts will often require that work be done through coalitions of groups that use the gifts and resources of each group to greatest advantage.

The Just Peace church understands that part of its prophetic ministry is calling forth the community of believers to witness to the gospel, but a complementary part of that ministry is confronting the iniquitous powers and principalities of the world. As such, prophetic voices must be raised that mobilize and empower people to resist injustice, while at the same time they challenge the power holders who dominate others. Such voices have proven that change can occur: Would Indians be free from British domination today without the prophetic witness of Mahatma Gandhi, who confronted injustice with nonviolent resistance? Would civil rights legislation have been enacted in the United States without the prophetic voice and witness of Martin Luther King Jr., who challenged institutions and laws that suppressed the rights of blacks? Would the atmospheric testing of atomic weapons or the tragedy of the Vietnam War have ended if the prophetic voice and witness of thousands of mothers and fathers had not been raised in a chorus of protest and confrontation?

Through prophetic acts of witness, the Just Peace church and its members claim their power to influence public and political will in a ministry of compassion for the world and to confirm the mission of the church and the sovereignty of God.

One of the significant outreach tasks of the Just Peace church is that of legislative advocacy. Americans have the gift of democracy and freedom, and it is a gift that should be handled responsibly and honored through its use. Influencing government, where decisions about social, economic, foreign, and military policies are made, is a basic right and key to solving many of the world's most serious problems. Members of the Just Peace church will exercise their right to vote at every opportunity; in addition, they will help others by participating in voter registration drives and supporting issues and candidate research. They will share their concerns with political decision makers and hold them accountable for positions taken during the legislative process.

The United Church of Christ, as a Just Peace church, needs to explore new and creative departures from traditional outreach activities. Examples include tax resistance and massive civil disobedience. While legislative advocacy is critical in shaping public policies, at times the demands of Just Peace call for acts of resistance. Had women not actively marched and picketed and blockaded the streets only a few decades ago, chances are they would not have gained the right to vote when they did. Had Rosa Parks tried introducing bills in Congress to reverse racial discrimination, chances are she would have ridden in the back of buses the rest of her life. Prophetic resistance is an important component of outreach activities.

Nonviolent resistance seeks to achieve justice through changing rather than conquering an "other." By nonviolently opposing existing injustices, acts of resistance dramatize issues and foster creative tensions such that the issues can no longer be ignored and must be confronted. Those who engage in acts of nonviolent resistance use them to arouse the conscience of the community over its injustices, to educate the public about alternatives, and to set in motion vast forces of positive social change. And for Christians, active resistance is an expression of deeply held faith.

Resistance methods and tactics may vary. They extend from simple protest and persuasion (e.g., distributing leaflets and marching), to noncooperation (e.g., boycotts, tax resistance, strikes, civil disobedience of unjust laws), to intervention (e.g., nonviolent blockades and obstruction and civil disobedience to unjust laws). Each method has its proper place and value in building a Just Peace.

Civil disobedience, the open and deliberate (usually nonviolent) violation of laws for political or social reasons, is a form of resistance. It is not to be confused with anarchism, which opposes all forms of institutionalized authority. The purpose of law is to maintain the structures and power balance in society, and, as such, Christians and non-Christians alike are generally law-abiding. But there are times when the integrity of people calls them to put their conscience or their faithfulness to God above the law. Civil disobedience is practiced as a conscientious response to faith principles and as a conscious strategy for social change.

Personal acts of faith and conscience are deeply connected to changes in public policy. The scope of draft resistance during the Vietnam War, for instance, affected the scope of U.S. military actions in Vietnam, as documented by Daniel Ellsberg in *The Pentagon Papers*. Civil disobedience can be a valuable tool for bringing about social change. It has been used successfully to secure workers' rights in the U.S. labor movement and to secure civil rights in the South beginning in the 1940s. And it has led to the overthrow of authoritarian regimes in several nations.

At times, prophetic acts of resistance by the Just Peace church are called for. Restraint must be exercised however: the goals of resistance acts must be clear, and the use of resistance as a strategy must be appropriate and not misused.

Outreach involves many other witnessing activities as well. Such witnessing can be done individually, within a congregation or the denomination, to other faith communities, or to the community at large.

Suggested Witness Outreach Activities for Just Peace

The following are suggestions for ways in which communities for faith can reach out to show their concern for life and their love of God through an uncompromising vision and witness to the wholeness of creation.

- Help develop the United Church of Christ Peace Advocacy Network and Hunger/Economic Justice Network, which seek change through legislative advocacy. Identify contact persons within the congregation and empower them to serve as leaders in mobilizing people for response on national legislative advocacy actions.
- Arrange for delegations of people to visit members of Congress, both to express their understanding of the solutions to pressing social problems and to influence the votes of the members of Congress so that humane and just legislation is enacted. Be persistent in expressing Just Peace views and alternatives.

- Set up letter-writing tables in a prominent place in the church building. Provide information on current legislation and addresses of members of Congress, and invite people to write before or after a meeting or worship service.
- Hold training workshops in political organizing and advocacy skills. Help people understand how public policy is formed and how it is changed. Use the workshops to generate support for the participation in coalitional work on legislative issues, as well as to develop further the UCC advocacy networks.
- Organize a candidates' forum prior to an election. Provide voter registration information and conduct a voter education campaign. Find out to whom candidates are beholden, where their power base lies, and who or what influences them the most. Determine the best course of action to help shape just public policies.
- Bring resolutions on Just Peace to congregational, association, and conference meetings. Use the resolutions to raise consciousness and provide an avenue of action. Provide background information with the resolutions and ask that time be set aside during the meetings for hearings on the resolutions so that people can grapple with different perceptions of issues and various strategies for effecting justice. Make certain that accountability is built into the resolution: who will do what by when and how it will be funded if expenditures of money are required.
- Set up tables with leaflets in local shopping centers and at fairs and libraries. Offer information and invite people to join with others in seeking Just Peace. Prepare displays and literature tables at Conference meetings. Be creative; use symbolic articles in the displays that will help people become aware of the issues and the experience of those suffering injustice

or oppression. Stacks of bread loaves next to empty plates or trash cans filled with luxury items could symbolize the affluence of the few as compared to the deprivation of the many; live plants could be used to symbolize and celebrate life and new growth; world globes wrapped with ribbon might symbolize our connectedness with brothers and sisters around the world, as well as the "gift" of creation.

- Organize and participate in demonstrations, prayer vigils, and other gatherings. Understand the purpose of the activity and use the methods most effective to achieve that purpose. Sponsor prayer breakfasts and dialogue times during meetings or before the regular workday begins in the morning. Use pilgrimages, processions, and "walk-a-thons" to raise the public's consciousness about Just Peace issues and as a witness by those involved. Involve all ages in making placards and banners for such events.

- Promote boycotts of products sold by companies that derive significant amounts of their income from military contracts. Withdraw investments from those companies—or use them through stockholder voting rights, to influence company decisions. Examine the investment portfolio of the church and see how it might exercise its corporate responsibility effectively.

- Covenant within the congregation to eliminate meat from the diet for one or more days each week. Meatless meals free grain, normally fed to livestock and poultry, for direct consumption. Exclude meat or poultry from church meals that are nutritious but simple and spare.

- Plant a vegetable garden on the church grounds. Share the produce grown with those in the community who have tended it; provide workshops on home gardening, including information on pest-control methods that do not damage the environment.

- Sponsor refugee families. Let others know of the joy—and the struggle—of reaching out and helping exiles in our land. Write or call the United Church Board for World Ministries to find out more about the need and opportunity for sponsoring refugees.
- Become a sanctuary church, providing refuge for those who illegally enter our nation seeking a safe haven from war, threat of death, and inhuman treatment. Study the theological, ethical, and legal issues involved in providing sanctuary to undocumented immigrants, letting the dialogue be aimed at discovering how to resolve conflict over differences in opinion about strategies for aiding undocumented immigrants and developing outreach programs that can involve the congregation. Support other congregations who are providing sanctuary and guide those who are not yet doing so.
- Assist non-English-speaking immigrants with cultural adjustments, language instruction, housing, employment, and other such needs.
- Open a food pantry for the needy or a shelter for the homeless. Support shelters for victims of family violence as well as half-way houses for those emerging from prison or on parole. Visit health and welfare centers to learn of problems that the dispossessed and poor must deal with; set goals and develop strategies for helping the congregation aid people as well as for empowering the poor to work for their own liberation.
- Explore how industry within the area is related to weapons production, and provide vocational counseling to those employed in weapons-related industries who wish to change jobs but are unskilled in other professions or cannot find other work. Provide pastoral care to those who have moral qualms about

the work they are engaged in and are seeking to resolve their moral dilemma.

- Study issues that involve resistance and civil disobedience—for example, providing sanctuary for undocumented immigrants, refusal to register for the draft, or refusal to pay taxes for war. Consider alternative actions and their consequences. Determine what special ministries the congregation will become involved in and how it will support people dealing with difficult moral and ethical questions related to civil disobedience. Find ways to provide for tax and draft counseling, legal assistance, pastoral support, and community support for such ministries and people.
- Minister to victims of war: families who still grieve over the loss of loved ones, individuals who have not learned to cope with the anger that came out of the Vietnam War, those still being maimed in wars around the world today. Develop ways of dealing with victims of war or militarism that restore them to wholeness, and work to prevent such tragedies in the future.
- Promote the special Peace Offering of the United Church of Christ within the congregation. Decide how and where the money retained by the congregation will be used to promote a Just Peace. Encourage other congregations to support joint projects that engage the skills and talents of each congregation.
- Examine the budget of the church. Reflect on how the congregation financially undergirds Just Peace ministries and if the congregation is a good steward of the gifts it has been given. Does it support Our Church's Wider Mission? Does it support other ministries within the denomination, Conference, or Association? Does it spend more on itself than it needs to? Are there ways to reduce the budgeted amount spent within the congregation by utilizing volunteered

skills and energies of groups and individuals? Are there purchases that can be postponed or eliminated to allow a greater share of the church's budget to be allocated to benevolent giving? Is there money in the church's investment portfolio that can be given to those in genuine need? If the church has more than it genuinely needs for its own operation, then it has that which belongs to someone else.

- Plan and hold a "Mission Fair" that tells of the mission and ministry of the church around the world. Use the fair to show where Christ's healing presence is needed and how the church is responding to needs throughout the world. Use it to promote solidarity with brothers and sisters from other cultures and nations; help show how people everywhere have the same basic needs. Help people to erase existing images of "enemy" by arranging for speakers and natives of other nations, especially those that are perceived as our "enemies." Seek to build understanding and trust.

- Produce a play that dramatizes the needs of the poor, the powerless, the disabled, youth. Advertise it within the congregation and wider community by using messages that inform as well as attract an audience. Or involve groups in street theater, at rallies or in front of federal buildings or offices of members of Congress, that symbolically dramatizes the threats to the world and offers hope and a vision of God's justice.

- Organize art displays and essay writing on Just Peace by and for children and youth. Reprint entries in the church newsletter so they can be shared with many people. Give entrants recognition with subscriptions to peace and justice journals or stationery with a peace motif on it.

- Design and create banners to hang in the church building. Use Bible themes and verses that raise consciousness. Share banners with other congregations; build connections within the United Church through such efforts.

- Distribute peace buttons and bumper stickers. Include them in the church newsletter. Enclose literature on Just Peace with the mailing.
- Run a newspaper advertisement or rent a billboard and let the public know of a position the congregation has taken on an issue. Use mass media to inform the public, invite action, and stimulate wider public debate.

Many suggested activities and actions have been included in this section. They are not intended as a prescription for programming but, rather, suggest ways in which the creative, life-giving, enriching work of building a Just Peace can be reflected in and through the life of the Just Peace church.

The urgency for peace in the world today calls for many dedicated people. But what is also needed is the vision and the creativity to continue to seek new understandings and new ways to build Just Peace. The Just Peace church, living in the presence of the Spirit, will continually explore and discover new possibilities for a Just Peace, so that God's mission in the world is fulfilled.

The church is indeed the Body of the Risen Christ. Through the grace of the Spirit, we perceive that the Word has become flesh in us—that in our midst, love is known, forgiveness is a reality, salvation is a hope ensured, and peace is a way of life. It is our calling to offer through service and even suffering the good news of reconciliation and atonement that God's realm of Just Peace holds forth for all the peoples of the world.

7. STRUCTURING THE UNITED CHURCH OF CHRIST FOR A JUST PEACE

"BLESSED ARE THE peacemakers, for they shall be called the children of God [Matt. 5:9]." In order to build and sustain Just Peace in the world, the organized efforts of many people will be required: peacemaking must be churchwide.

At the national level, the United Church of Christ has been engaged in major efforts to secure a Just Peace. But if Just Peace is to be a significant witness to our whole denomination, a peacemaking, justice-seeking community needs to be developed at local, regional, national, and international levels to nurture and support Just Peace efforts by people throughout the church and the world. At each of these levels the United Church of Christ must begin to structure itself, in such a way that the people of God are prepared, individually and corporately, to be agents and advocates of a Just Peace.

Much of the "structuring" to be done within the United Church of Christ is surely less than a mechanical flow chart or table of tasks and responsibilities and staff positions. It is more of a conversion, a *metanoia*, a change of heart and will. It is rescuing "peacemaking" from being seen only as something that one "does." A peacemaker, conceived biblically, refers not only to something that one *does* but to something that one *is*. Peacemaking is descriptive of the being, the life, of God's people. And witnessing events or acts arise out of that *being* as an expression and outlet of life and faith; it is the genesis, not the consequence, of acts that give substance to us as Christians. If our denomination and we, as its members, take on issues only to preserve ourselves or the world and not because we are genuinely concerned servants and stewards, if we conjure up parades and rallies and offerings without being grasped by Word and Deed, then no amount of "works" will alter the world or the church in our history. Much of the structuring to be done in our church today is to be a seeking of the best ways to empower and enable people to discover the call to be peacemakers, that the Holy Spirit can increasingly flourish in our midst.

At this point, with new possibilities not clearly revealed to us, remolding the United Church of Christ is less a restructuring than it is a directed pointing to a Just Peace as the heart of our life together. The implications of such a directed pointing are clear: national instrumentalities and bodies must find new ways of relating to one another and focusing their work; local congregations and associations and conferences must explore how they can each make a difference in the world, how they can more faithfully and effectively respond to the call to build a Just Peace; and funding patterns within the whole church may change. But church polity will not change overnight; autonomy will not slowly slither away into some quiet grave; the myths of our church and world will not suddenly be overcome with explosive insight. There is much to be torn down, much to be built up, much to be rendered anew through our living together and witnessing together on a journey that seeks to give new substance and meaning to our common faith.

Congregations

At the local level, there must be a community of agents and advocates of Just Peace. Local congregations, as the fundamental unit of peacemaking within the life of the United Church of Christ, need to organize themselves and train themselves to make a difference on issues of Just Peace both within and beyond the walls of the church. Congregations have essential roles in providing support for Just Peace efforts at the local level. In their worship, education, outreach, and funding efforts, local congregations help to build the community of agents and advocates of Just Peace and help support the efforts of those at other levels.

Congregations can help the Just Peace community, shape public will, and build the political will that gives flesh to the vision of wholeness for the world. Through its worship, the congregation is empowered and sustained for its mission. Through education, the congregation is provided with information needed to determine goals and strategies. Through outreach projects and programs, the congregation is enabled to witness to the faith and becomes the active advocate of Just Peace. Through funding, the congregation supports its own Just Peace ministries and those of others, including the wider church.

One of the important tasks within the congregation is that of building the community of Just Peace makers, which involves more than just building an organization. Building an organization involves recruiting people to do tasks, but building the community involves consciously cultivating and maintaining the bonds that make the group of gathered witnesses vital, healthy, growing, and dynamic. In community, we know ourselves and others as persons of hope and creativity, as well as persons of fear, injustice, and potential violence. In community, we can identify the powers of death within us and our society that must be resisted. And in community, we discover signs of new birth and life that are to be affirmed and nurtured. With community, a sense of solidarity pervades the group; there is a sense of common striving toward an obtainable goal. There is also a sense of working together to reach that goal.

Just as community needs to be built, so does organization. Goal setting and strategy planning, action and reflection, need to be done within and beyond the congregation so that it can become an effective agent and advocate for Just Peace. Peacemaking task forces or committees within each congregation should be established; they become the vehicles for planning and implementing, coordinating and evaluating, the Just Peace ministries of the congregation. The peacemaking task force or committee, along with other groups within the congregation, develops the skills within individuals and the corporate body that are needed to build a Just Peace.

Each congregation should also have members who are involved in the United Church of Christ Peace Advocacy Network and the Hunger/Economic Justice Network. Through these networks, members are informed of current and pending national legislation, and rapid response on Just Peace issues before Congress can be generated within the congregation.

Congregations should be encouraged to develop a Just Peace covenant, which lifts up the various elements of Just Peace as they relate to worship, prayer, Bible study, education, organizing, advocacy, and financial support. This covenant can be renewed annually to give specific expression to the peacemaking tasks the congregation sees before it each year.

And finally, congregations, new and old communities for a Just Peace, should be known by the world for their life-style of peace with justice: come and see these Christians, for they live, personally and corporately and in the world, as justice-filled peacemakers! See how they love one another; see how they love the world! See how they strive for justice for the oppressed; see how they struggle against despair and poverty and hunger and death! See how they have given up an obsession with power and material wealth, how they share their hearts and souls and energy with others! See how they pit themselves against the overwhelming forces of death! See how these Christians hope!

Conferences and Associations

If Just Peace is to be built, the sustained involvement of grass-roots activity is essential. Conferences and Associations must sustain local efforts that support Just Peace community, education, organizing, and advocacy. The United Church of Christ, if it is to take its work seriously as a Just Peace church, must develop strong regional centers that sustain work at the grass-roots level while at the same time carrying out Just Peace ministries from the regional level.

As in local congregations, Associations and Conferences must have the making of peace and justice in their lifeblood and heartbeats. Here, too, in its professional staff and leadership, the making of peace and justice grows out of faith in the power of the Risen Christ and must be identified, owned, and lived as vital to the life of an individual and the Association and Conference.

The quality of leadership within the Conference or Association is critical if Just Peace ministries are to affect the structure of Conferences and Associations in *all* of their dimensions. Staff persons and members of boards of directors and committees and task forces must all embrace Just Peace within their focus. Association and Conference overviews and plans for Just Peace ministries need to be developed and implemented, and accountability must be agreed upon. Conferences and Associations must work together to evaluate continually their structure, envisioning new models more viable for the age they live in.

A variety of options are possible for Just Peace ministries at the Association and Conference level.

- Develop regional United Church of Christ peace centers that provide resources for local and national groups through educational, organization, advocacy, and funding efforts.
- Fund part-time, contract, or full-time Just Peace staff at the Association or Conference level, which tie educational and organizing work more closely to the life of the churches.
- Fund ecumenical peace staff in states or major metropolitan areas where the work of Conferences or Associations could be carried out jointly with other denominations.
- Develop communications, internal and ecumenical, that continually link faith, peace, and justice.
- Use mass media to advocate Just Peace issues.
- Model Just Peace through the life-style of the Conference or Association—its personnel practices, systems of accountability, budgeting, purchasing, investments, and stewardship of property and people.

- The Church and Ministry Committee and Conference and National leadership could work with UCC-related seminaries to integrate more fully the making of peace with justice into the life of the seminary.
- Association Church and Ministry Committees might begin to develop standards and guidelines that encourage candidates for the ordained ministry to seek academic and experiential backgrounds in peace and justice theology, education, and action. Many Associations now require CPE (clinical pastoral education) for ordination; perhaps in the future, a commitment to peacemaking might be of equal value.
- Conferences and Associations could provide training opportunities for local church leaders to explore and support new thought patterns and life-styles.
- Conferences can support conscientious objectors to war by maintaining files and helping to document claims to such status; likewise, they can support tax resisters by establishing escrow accounts for those who withhold payment of taxes based upon a protest against the funding of nuclear and biochemical weapons that individuals feel represents immoral complicity in their use.

The Conference is an important link between the National Instrumentalities and local churches. In partnership, the Conference interprets, supports, and disseminates the work of the United Church of Christ at the national and global level while communicating and advocating its perception of the needs of society, local churches, and Conference to the appropriate National Instrumentality. The work of the Conference, as well as that of the Associations, must be supported by local congregations as well as by National Instrumentalities—and vice versa.

National Instrumentalities and Other Bodies

Again, a Just Peace must permeate the lifeblood of the offices and staff of the church at the national level. The United Church of Christ must not only make claim of itself as a Just Peace church; it must take claim of that identity. And such a claiming must be done fully by all of the instrumentalities and bodies of the United Church of Christ. Just Peace issues cannot be placed solely in the possession of the Office for Church in Society, just as fighting racism cannot be assigned solely to the Commission for Racial Justice or fighting sexism thrust solely into the hands of the Coordinating Center for Women.

Our Instrumentalities, separately and together, need to identify with the work of Just Peace at the national level and then together negotiate tasks and functions appropriate for each. As negotiations take place, peacemaking begins and creative partnerships are envisioned and developed.

Until such time as new partnerships and structures are formed, a descriptive division of tasks and responsibilities is helpful. Such a description follows.

THE OFFICE FOR CHURCH IN SOCIETY

The Office for Church in Society (OCIS) should provide national coordination for the Just Peace ministries of the United Church of Christ. At least one half of the funds from a yearly peacemaking offering should go to OCIS, with OCIS working with the other National Instrumentalities to direct these funds to the most effective Just Peace activities among national, regional, and ecumenical bodies.

OCIS should also assume responsibility for developing and empowering the whole church as agents and advocates of Just Peace. Such empowerment includes coordinating support for the peacemaking and justice-making community and coordinating Just Peace advocacy efforts.

OCIS has a special role to play in peace advocacy. Effective advocacy will require direct lobbying efforts in Washington and organizing, supporting, and mobilizing a grass-roots peace advocacy network with contact people coordinating these networks in each state and in as many Congressional districts and local congregations as possible. Just Peace advocacy will also require effective use of the communications media, which will need coordination between the Washington OCIS Office, the Office of Communication, and the UCC President's Office.

An essential component of effective Just Peace efforts is the development of theological statements, public policy analysis, and special position papers and proposals, including long-term social analysis of new approaches to world peace. OCIS should have the capacity for such efforts.

THE UNITED CHURCH BOARD FOR WORLD MINISTRIES

The United Church Board for World Ministries (UCBWM), because of its global relationships, has a vital role to play in Just Peace ministries. Our partner churches around the world are increasingly sending us the message that rather than money or missionaries they need the addressing of the politics of violence and injustice; these partner churches perceive that many of their problems orginate with U.S. foreign and military policy.

The UCBWM needs to help U.S. churches hear this critique and develop, with our partner churches, effective peacemaking programs across national boundaries, helping to build the global community for making Just Peace.

THE UNITED CHURCH BOARD FOR HOMELAND MINISTRIES

The United Church Board for Homeland Ministries (UCBHM) should assume responsibility for developing Just Peace educational resources, working closely with the Office for Church in Society so that these resources are connected to the Just Peace advocacy and Just Peace organizing strategies of the denomination.

In its work with the family-life priority of the denomination, the UCBHM should continue their work of helping families work together as a unit for Just Peace concerns and to live in justice and peace themselves.

Two special areas of work for the UCBHM include the seeking of economic justice among the poor of this nation (including developing the connection between economic justice at home and military aggression abroad) and supporting ministries of higher education. Campus ministers and church-related colleges have special responsibilities in seeing that the search for global peace is addressed in colleges and universities.

THE OFFICE OF COMMUNICATION

The Office of Communication should support the denomination in making its public witness effective in mass media. Because the advocacy efforts of the OCIS and the peace and hunger/economic justice advocacy networks have need of effective use of the media, close

coordination is required with the Office of
Communication.

The Stewardship Council should be responsible for
interpreting and promoting an annual Just Peace
Offering. The promotion of this offering will include
interpreting the Just Peace ministry of the United
Church of Christ to local congregations. The offering
receipts should be divided in such a way that
Conferences and congregations may each retain 25
percent of the offering to support their own Just Peace
ministries. The remainder of the offering receipts (50
percent) is to be forwarded to the OCIS for national Just
Peace ministries, including work by the OCIS, work by
other National Instrumentalities and bodies,
ecumenical work, and grants to peacemaking
organizations and programs.

The unique division of the offering reinforces the
churchwide nature of building a Just Peace and
provides congregations, Conferences, and
Instrumentalities with money to do their tasks. The
offering will be promoted by the Stewardship Council
out of a budget negotiated by the Council and the OCIS
from funds received in the offering.

In addition, the Stewardship Council should
continue to develop resources that enable people to
discover alternative life-styles that promote the greater
sharing of all that we have and are.

THE COMMISSION FOR RACIAL JUSTICE

The Commission for Racial Justice (CRJ) should
assume responsibility for developing the linkages

among racial and social justice, economic justice, and global justice. The CRJ will be instrumental in helping all parts of the church and society to see the relationship among security, justice, order, and equality.

The Office for Church Life and Leadership

The Office for Church Life and Leadership should develop resources for church leaders, helping to identify and support the qualities of leadership that make for effective efforts to achieve justice and peace.

The Office of President

The Office of President should serve as the primary speaker for the prophetic role of the church and as the primary pastor to the whole church in nurturing its justice and peacemaking efforts.

Our Life

The church is the Body of the Risen Christ; through this vessel of the Spirit we bear witness to the realm of God. Through the church, we gather in community to build a Just Peace, our understanding of God's will for creation. While Just Peace has not completely evidenced itself in the world today, it is our calling as individuals and as the church to act and pray for its full presence. We understand this to have the following implications for our life together and for our witness as a fellowship.

124

1. We affirm diversity and inclusivity in faith expressions within our membership, for we each "see as in a mirror darkly."
2. We reject any absolutizing of faith experience—be it the patristic writings of the first and second centuries, or the sixteenth-century Reformation, or a twentieth-century liberation movement—as the ultimate test of religious purity and true doctrine.
3. We affirm that "God has many whom the Church does not have"; that the Spirit moves through many channels and vessels, both secular and religious.
4. We recommit ourselves to the rich heritage of ecumenicity that is ours within the United Church of Christ, mindful that Christ calls us not to build or maintain a denominational institution but to witness to and participate in the realm of God, Just Peace, which is at hand.
5. We affirm our calling to incarnate Just Peace in our life-styles as individuals and corporate bodies, including the following:
   a. nonhierarchical structures
   b. nonviolence in word and deed in relationships among persons of all ages, groups, and nations
   c. confession that we have been a support for violence that has oppressed the earth and its people and that we have sanctioned and condoned war
   d. just relationships among members, churches, and Instrumentalities, specifically as that entails the distribution of material resources.
6. We commit ourselves to shape our congregational life so that it
   a. provides worship that helps center our lives in the reality of the Just Peace that is the good news of Jesus Christ

b. encourages members to receive the gift of God's Just Peace in their lives and through prayer, Bible study, and action, empowers members to become peacemakers in today's world
c. enables and equips members to grow as peacemakers in their families, congregations, and communities
d. equips the people of God for work for social, racial, and economic justice and to respond to people caught in poverty and despair, joining with them in their struggle
e. encourages the congregation to support world efforts toward human rights and economic justice, with the possibility of focusing on a specific area such as Central America, East Asia, the Middle East, the United States, or southern Africa
f. becomes an effective agent of change in ending the arms race, reversing the worldwide growth of militarism, and reducing tensions among nations
g. sets up a Just Peace Committee or some other action group that will lead the congregation in its peacemaking efforts
h. selects two or three members to serve as contact people for the Peace Advocacy Network and the Hunger/Economic Justice Network, working with congressional district organizers to seek Just Peace in the political order
i. supports the churchwide peacemaking efforts of the United Church of Christ through financial gifts to the annual all-church Just Peace Offering, UCC Peace Fund, Hunger Action Fund, Neighbors in Need, and other such means.

7. Recognizing that the Just Peace church views the state as an order responsible for the establishment of social justice and human welfare and views its own

role as one of calling the state to task when it does not make justice its first priority, and recognizing that the United States has a unique role to play in moving toward global structures of Just Peace, we accept our responsibility for the political order and our role in transforming national and international governmental structures into structures that move toward Just Peace.

8. Recognizing that systemic violence and systemic injustice have become ingrained in global governmental structures, we call for extraordinary witness as well as ordinary political involvement to break the power of structural evil and move toward greater embodiment of Just Peace. Therefore:

   a. We urge our young members to consider becoming conscientious objectors to war, refusing to enter military service, until such time as our nation is openly attacked by another nation. While we acknowledge a role for the military in our nation, we also witness that this role has become distorted and that extraordinary witness is needed to challenge our nation into rethinking the role of military power in the world today.

   b. Because nuclear and biochemical weapons represent such a crime against humanity and because of the urgency of halting production of new systems, we encourage and stand in solidarity with all in our membership and outside who refuse to accept employment with any project related to nuclear and biochemical weapons and warfare.

   c. Because the use of biochemical and nuclear weapons stands outside all moral possibility, we encourage all in our membership and outside who serve in the armed forces to refuse any and all orders to use such weapons.

9. Because the times call for renewed and intense efforts at political involvement to establish the conditions of Just Peace, as well as nonviolent direct actions to witness to the political order that is not moving fast enough toward justice and peace, we call upon our members who choose primarily political involvement to accept and support those who choose civil disobedience as essential prophetic witness. We also call upon our members who move toward civil disobedience and prophetic witness to support those who recognize that the primary task is the political task of developing a just and peaceful political order.

Summary

Can the international economic system be made more equitable?

Can the arms race be stopped?

What role should the church play in this process?

These are massive questions. But as we seek to answer them, one conclusion seems clear: the United States, as the most powerful economic and technological force in the world, has a decisive role to play. While peace and justice require support from all nations, and no one nation can achieve them by itself, the United States is in a strategic position to take critical initiatives that will transform the current systemic injustice and terror.

This means that the churches in the United States have a special and most critical calling. The future of humanity may well rest on whether the churches can create in our nation the passion to care about the poor and the global terror enough to take new steps to change the course of history. The churches must have clarity on this calling: we are called by God to preach the gospel of peace and compassion with such intensity that nations repent and turn, and history is changed.

God is calling upon the churches. God's calling to them is highly political. God calls the churches to become involved in the political process, the politics of a Just Peace.

The churches of the United States are timid. While churches in most times and places have understood that they have a political role to play in society, those in the United States take the separation of church and state very seriously. They have great hesitancy in entering the political arena.

Fundamentalists and television evangelists, on the one hand, have recently taken great strides into the political arena, but often they are to urge government enforcement of private morality and individual religious piety. Where the religious political right has spoken politically about peace and justice, it has sounded more like war propaganda from crusaders who identify the forces of Communism with the forces of Satan, urging military defeat in a cosmic battle.

The Catholic Church, on the other hand, has been providing a tremendous witness to peace in the last few years. The Bishops' Pastoral Letter on War and Peace has reshaped the debate on arms control at the national level and has forced the White House and the Pentagon to take the witness of the Catholic Church seriously. The Bishops' Pastoral Letter on Catholic Social Teaching and the U.S. Economy places the Church squarely on the side of the poor. And the role the Church is playing in the Central American conflict has done much to shape and restrain U.S. response.

Mainline Protestant churches have been slow to enter the political debate in large numbers. Many in the churches have not sensed the importance of this mission.

True, peace has been at or near the center of the mainline churches' life over the past few years. And the United Church of Christ has taken enormous strides into the politics of peace, both in Washington and in developing grass-roots advocacy networks. But most denominations, while active at peace education and peace witness, have been reluctant and slow to enter the political arena at the national level. For most of them, there is not adequate consensus that political ministry is both appropriate and essential.

Within the United Church of Christ there is a good deal of support for the involvement of the church in the political process. We expect the church to take moral leadership. We understand the role of the church as a transforming agent in society. We know that justice and peace are religious concepts as well as political processes, and we expect the church to be engaged in the political struggle for justice and peace. Our differences center mainly on how to go about the creation of a Just Peace.

Because the United Church of Christ has perhaps the greatest support for the involvement of the church in the political process, we have a special leadership responsibility. Ours is the task of exploring new models that will help the church to be politically effective in the creation of a Just Peace within the framework of the First Amendment. We must create these models within our own denomination, and we must reach out to other churches in creating ecumenical models.

In defining a Just Peace, or shalom, as the presence and interrelation of friendship, justice, and common security from violence, we commit ourselves to seek these goals. It is the task of our nation, and all nations of the world, to structure themselves so as to produce friendship, justice, and common security from violence.

In the Pronouncement, which was passed by General Synod XV and which forms the next chapter of this book, we have attempted to spell out how a Just Peace might be achieved. We have attempted to move from belief to policy.

This policy cannot claim to be infallible. It can claim to be the best wisdom of many Christians who have struggled for months and years in the process of creating a General Synod Pronouncement. It can claim the right to be taken seriously as one expression of the Spirit at one point in time as Christians struggle to develop the ideas and policies that will move our nation and our world toward that interrelation of friendship, justice, and common security. If it is fallible, then we need to be about the task of discovering its fallibility and of developing new policies that will bring us a Just Peace.

8.

GENERAL SYNOD XV: PRONOUNCEMENT AND PROPOSAL

PRONOUNCEMENT: AFFIRMING THE UNITED CHURCH OF CHRIST AS A JUST PEACE CHURCH

I. Summary

Affirms the United Church of Christ to be a Just Peace church and defines Just Peace as the interrelation of friendship, justice, and common security from violence. Places the UCC General Synod in opposition to the institution of war.

II. Background

The Thirteenth General Synod called upon the United Church to become a peace church, and the

---

Chapter 8 may be reprinted as a public document of the church provided that it is credited to General Synod XV.

Fourteenth General Synod asked a Peace Theology Development Team to recommend to the Fifteenth General Synod theology, policy, and structure for enabling the United Church to be a peacemaking church. This pronouncement is based on insights from all three of the historic approaches of Christians to issues of war and peace—pacifism, just war, and crusade—but attempts to move beyond these traditions to an understanding rooted in the vision of shalom, linking peace and justice. Since the just-war criterion itself now rules out war under modern conditions, it is imperative to move beyond just-war thinking to the theology of a Just Peace.

III. Biblical and Theological Foundations

A Just Peace is grounded in God's activity in *creation*. Creation shows the desire of God to sustain the world and not destroy. The creation anticipates what is to come: the history-long relationship between God and humanity and the coming vision of shalom.

Just Peace is grounded in *covenant* relationship. God creates and calls us into covenant, God's gift of friendship. "I will make a covenant of peace with them; it shall be an everlasting covenant with them; and I will bless them and multiply them, and will set my sanctuary in the midst of them for evermore [Ezek. 37:26]." When God's abiding presence is embraced, human well-being results, or *shalom*, which can be translated *Just Peace*. A Just Peace is grounded in the reconciling activity of *Jesus Christ*. Human sin is the rejection of the covenant of friendship with God and one another and the creation and perpetuation of structures of evil. Through God's own suffering love on the cross, the power of these structures has been broken and the possibility of relationship restored.

A Just Peace is grounded in the presence of the *Holy Spirit*. God sends the Holy Spirit to continue the struggle to overcome the powers ranged against human bonding. Thus our hope for a Just Peace does not rest on human efforts alone but on God's promise that we will "have life and have it abundantly [John 10:10]."

A Just Peace is grounded in the community of reconciliation: the Just Peace *church*. Jesus, who is our peace (Ephesians 2:14), performed signs of forgiveness and healing and made manifest that God's reign is for those who are in need. The church is a continuation of that servant manifestation. As a Just Peace church, we embody a Christ fully engaged in human events. The church is thus a real countervailing power to those forces which divide, which perpetuate human enmity and injustice, which destroy.

Just Peace is grounded in *hope*. Shalom is the vision which pulls all creation toward a time when weapons are swept off the earth and all creatures lie down together without fear, where all have their own fig tree and dwell secure from want. As Christians, we offer this conviction to the world: peace is possible.

IV. Statement of Christian Conviction

A. The Fifteenth General Synod affirms a Just Peace as the presence and interrelation of friendship, justice, and common security from violence. The General Synod affirms the following as marks of a Just Peace theology:

Peace is *possible*. A Just Peace is a basic gift of God and is the force and vision moving human history.

135

The *meaning* of a Just Peace and God's activity in human history is understood through the Bible, church history, and the voices of the oppressed and those in struggle for justice and peace.

Nonviolent *conflict* is a normal and healthy reflection of diversity; working through conflict constructively should lead to growth of both individuals and nations.

Nonviolence is a Christian response to conflict shown to us by Jesus. We have barely begun to explore this little-known process of reconciliation.

Violence can and must be minimized, even eliminated, in most situations. However, because evil and violence are embedded in human nature and institutions, they will remain present in some form.

War can and must be eliminated.

The *state* should be based upon participatory consent and should be primarily responsible for developing justice and well-being, enforcing the law, and minimizing violence in the process.

International structures of friendship, justice, and common security from violence are necessary and possible at this point in history in order to eliminate the institution of war and move toward a Just Peace.

Unexpected initiatives of friendship and reconciliation can transform interpersonal and international relationships and are essential to restoring community.

B. The Fifteenth General Synod affirms the United Church of Christ as a Just Peace church. The General Synod affirms the following marks of a Just Peace church, calling upon each local church to become:

A community of hope, believing a Just Peace is possible, working toward this end, and communicating to the larger world the excitement and possibility of a Just Peace.

A community of worship and celebration, centering its identity in justice and peacemaking and the good news of peace, which is Jesus Christ.

A community of biblical and theological reflection, studying the scriptures, the Christian story, and the working of the Spirit in the struggle against injustice and oppression.

A community of spiritual nurture and support, loving one another and giving one another strength in the struggle for a Just Peace.

A community of honest and open conflict, a zone of freedom where differences may be expressed, explored, and worked through in mutual understanding and growth.

A community of empowerment, renewing and training people for making peace and doing justice.

A community of financial support, developing programs and institutions for a Just Peace.

A community of solidarity with the poor, seeking to be present in places of oppression, poverty, and violence and standing with the oppressed in the struggle to resist and change this evil.

A community of loyalty to God and to the whole human community over any nation or rival idolatry.

A community without enemies, willing to risk and be vulnerable, willing to take surprising initiatives to transform situations of enmity.

A community of repentance, confessing its own guilt and involvement in structural injustice and violence, ready to acknowledge its entanglement in evil, seeking to turn toward new life.

A community of resistance, standing against social structures comfortable with violence and injustice.

A community of sacrifice and commitment, ready to go the extra mile, and then another mile, in the search for justice and peace.

A community of political and social engagement, in regular dialogue with the political order, participating in peace and justice advocacy networks, witnessing to a Just Peace in the community and in the nation, joining the social and political struggle to implement a Just Peace.

C. The Fifteenth General Synod affirms friendship as essential to a Just Peace.

1. We affirm the unity of the whole human community and oppose any use of nationalism to divide this covenant of friendship.

2. We reject all labeling of others as enemies and the creation of institutions that perpetuate enemy relations.

3. We affirm diversity among peoples and nations and the growth and change that can emerge from the interchange of differing value systems, ideologies, religions, and political and economic systems.

4. We affirm nonviolent conflict as inevitable and valuable, an expression of diversity that is essential to healthy relationships among people and nations.

5. We affirm all nations developing global community and interchange, including:
   a. freedom of travel;
   b. free exchange of ideas and open dialogue;
   c. scientific, cultural, and religious exchanges;

d. public education that portrays the other nations fairly, breaking down enemy stereotypes and images;

e. knowledge of foreign languages.

D. The Fifteenth General Synod affirms justice as essential to a Just Peace.

1. We affirm all nations working together to ensure that people everywhere will be able to meet their basic needs, including the right of every person to:

a. food and clean water;

b. adequate health care;

c. decent housing;

d. meaningful employment;

e. basic education;

f. participation in community decision making and the political process;

g. freedom of worship and religious expression;

h. protection from torture;

i. protection of rights without regard to race, sex, sexual orientation, religion, or national or social origin.

2. We affirm the establishment of a more just international order in which:

a. trade barriers, tariffs and debt burdens do not work against the interests of the poor and developing nations;

b. poor nations have a greater share in the policies and management of global economic institutions.

3. We affirm economic policies which target aid to the most needy: the rural poor, women, nations with poor natural resources or structural problems, and the poor within each nation.

4. We affirm economic policies which will further the interests of the poor within each nation:

a. promoting popular participation;
b. empowering the poor to make effective demands on social systems;
c. encouraging decentralization and greater community control;
d. providing for the participation of women in development;
e. redistributing existing assets, including land, and distributing more equitably future benefits of growth;
f. reducing current concentrations of economic and political power;
g. providing for self-reliant development, particularly in food production.
5. We affirm nations transferring funds from military expenditures into programs which will aid the poor, and developing strategies of converting military industries to Just Peace industries.
6. We oppose the injustices resulting from the development of national-security states that currently repress the poor in organizing society against an external enemy.
7. We affirm a free and open press within each nation, without hindrance from government.

E. The Fifteenth General Synod affirms common security from violence as essential to a Just Peace.
1. We affirm that national security includes four interrelated components:
a. provision for general well-being;
b. cultivation of justice;
c. provision for defense of a nation;
d. creation of political atmosphere and structure in which a Just Peace can flourish and the risk of war is diminished or eliminated.

2. We affirm the right and obligations of governments to use civil authority to prevent lawlessness and protect human rights. Such force must not be excessive and must always be in the context of the primary responsibility of the state in creating social justice and promoting human welfare. Any use of force or coercion must be based on the participatory consent of the people.

3. We affirm that war must be eliminated as an instrument of national policy and the global economy must be more just. To meet these goals, international institutions must be strengthened.

4. We affirm our support for the United Nations, which should be strengthened by developing the following:

   a. more authority in disputes among countries;
   b. peacekeeping forces, including a permanent force of at least 5,000, able to police border disputes and intervene when called to do so by the United Nations;
   c. peacemaking teams, trained in mediation, conflict intervention, and conflict resolution;
   d. support for international peace academies;
   e. a global satellite surveillance system to provide military intelligence to the common community;
   f. international agreements to limit military establishments and the international arms trade;
   g. an international ban on the development, testing, use, and possession of nuclear and biochemical weapons of mass destruction;
   h. an international ban on all weapons in space and all national development of space-based defensive systems and Strategic Defense Initiatives.

5. We affirm our support for the International Court of Justice and for the strengthening of international law, including:
   a. the Law of the Sea Treaty;
   b. universal ratification of the international covenants and conventions which seek to implement the Universal Declaration of Human Rights;
   c. recognition of the jurisdiction of the International Court of Justice and removal of restrictions, such as the Connally Amendment, which impair the Court's effective functioning.
6. We reject any use of threat to use weapons and forces of mass destruction and any doctrine of deterrence based primarily on using such weapons. We also reject unilateral full-scale disarmament as a currently acceptable path out of the present international dilemma. We affirm the development of new policies of common security, using a combination of negotiated agreements, new international institutions and institutional power, nonviolent strategies, unilateral initiatives to lessen tensions, and new policies which will make the global economy more just.
7. We affirm the mutual and verifiable freeze on the testing, production, and deployment of nuclear weapons as the most important step in breaking the escalating dynamics of the arms race, and call upon the United States and the Soviet Union and other nations to take unilateral initiatives toward implementing such a freeze, contingent upon the other side responding, until such a time as a comprehensive freeze can be negotiated.
8. We declare our opposition to all weapons of mass destruction. All nations should:

a. declare that they will never use such weapons;
b. cease immediately the testing, production, and deployment of nuclear weapons;
c. begin dismantling these arsenals;
d. while the process of dismantling is going on, negotiate comprehensive treaties banning all such future weapons by any nation.
9. We declare our opposition to war, violence, and terrorism. All nations should:
    a. declare that they will never attack another nation;
    b. make unilateral initiatives toward dismantling their military arsenals, calling upon other nations to reciprocate;
    c. develop mechanisms for international law, international peacekeeping, and international conflict resolution.

A PROPOSAL FOR ACTION: ORGANIZING THE UNITED CHURCH OF CHRIST AS A JUST PEACE CHURCH

I. Summary

Affirms the United Church of Christ to be a Just Peace church and defines Just Peace as the interrelation of friendship, justice, and common security from violence. Places the UCC General Synod in opposition to the institution of war.

II. Background

This Proposal for Action builds on the proposed Pronouncement, also submitted to the Fifteenth General Synod, "Affirming the United Church of Christ as a Just Peace Church." Like the Pronouncement, the Proposal for Action has been developed in response to the request of the Fourteenth General Synod to recommend theology, policy, and structure for enabling the United Church to be a peacemaking church.

III. Directional Statement

The Fifteenth General Synod calls upon all in the United Church of Christ to recognize that the creating of a Just Peace is central to their identity as Christians and to their baptism into the Christian community.

IV. Call to Local Churches

The Fifteenth General Synod calls on local churches to organize their common life so as to make a difference in the achieving of a Just Peace and the ending of the institution of war.

The Fifteenth General Synod calls for the development of four key components within local churches: spiritual development, Just Peace education, political advocacy, and community witness.

    1. We call all local churches to the inward journey of spiritual nurture: prayer for a Just Peace, study of the scriptures, theological reflection upon the work of the Holy Spirit, and celebration and worship that center the life of the community in the power and

reality of the God who creates a Just Peace.
We call for the development of Christian
community that nurtures and supports
members in the search for a Just Peace. We
commend to all local churches the use of the
World Peace Prayer, using the example of the
Benedictine Sisters, who pray this specific
prayer each day at noon:
Lead me (us) from death to life, from
    falsehood to truth.
Lead me (us) from despair to hope, from fear
    to trust.
Lead me (us) from hate to love, from war to
    peace.
Let peace fill our hearts, our world, our
    universe.

2. We call all local churches to the inward
    journey of education. Knowing that there are
    no easy answers to the creating of a Just
    Peace, we call for churches to establish the
    climate where all points of view can be
    respected, all honest feelings and opinions
    shared in the search for new answers and
    directions. We call for a steady program of
    Just Peace education, a steady flow of
    information on Just Peace issues into the life
    of the congregation.

3. We call all local churches to the outward
    journey of political witness, enabling all
    members to join the search for the politics of
    a Just Peace. Just Peace is both a religious
    concept and a political concept, and
    participation in the political arena is
    essential. We call for each church to appoint
    a contact person for the UCC Peace
    Advocacy and Hunger/Economic Justice

Networks to follow closely those political issues most critical to the development of a Just Peace and to alert members of the local church when it is most appropriate to write or contact their Senators and Representatives.

4. We call all local churches to the outward journey of community witness. We call for local churches to make their convictions known in their communities through public forums, media, and presence in the public arena. We call for local churches to help shape public opinion and the climate in which the issues of a Just Peace are shaped. We call for churches to explore with military industries the opportunities for conversion into Just Peace industries. We call for evangelistic outreach, inviting others to join in the search for a Just Peace.

Because the times are so critical, we call for extraordinary witness as well as ordinary political involvement to break the power of the structural evils which prevent a Just Peace. We call upon local churches to be understanding and even supportive of persons who out of individual conscience take the responsibility for such nonviolent extraordinary witness. Examples of such witness might include: becoming a conscientious objector to war; refusing acceptance of employment with any project related to nuclear and biochemical weapons and warfare; refusing any and all assignments to use weapons of mass destruction as a member of the military; withholding tax money in protest against the

excessively militaristic policies of our
government; and engaging in acts of
nonviolent civil disobedience, willingly
going to jail to call attention to specific
outrages.

V. Call to Conferences and National Bodies

The Fifteenth General Synod calls upon
Conferences and national bodies of the United Church
of Christ to organize their common life so as to make a
difference in the achieving of a Just Peace and the
ending of the institution of war.

The Fifteenth General Synod calls for the
development of four key components in developing the
United Church of Christ so that it can make a real
difference over the next years: regional centers,
Washington advocacy, international presence, and
national programs.

1. We call upon Conferences to develop regional
   centers able to link local churches into effective
   regional and national strategies. A variety of
   options are possible at the Association and
   Conference levels.
   - The development of regional UCC peace
     centers that provide resources to local groups
     through educational, organizational, advocacy,
     and funding efforts;
   - The development of ecumenical, regional Just
     Peace centers, in partnership with other
     denominations;
   - The funding of part-time, contract, or full-time
     Just Peace staff for the Association or
     Conference;

- The funding of ecumenical peace staff in states or metropolitan areas.
2. We call for the strengthening of our advocacy work in Washington, DC, with more funding to develop the capacity of the United Church of Christ to make its witness known in the national political arena, to expand its capacity for policy analysis, to increase its presence on Capitol Hill in shaping legislation, to develop stronger communication links with churches around the country, to share political developments and urge action, and to build coalitions.
3. We call upon the United Church of Christ Board for World Ministries to explore and develop new models of peace and justice ministries globally to address particular situations of injustice, oppression, and real or potential violence, and to develop communication links between Christians in these critical situations and Christians in the United States, developing global partnership and global awareness in the search for a Just Peace.
4. We call upon all national bodies to develop effective programs of advocacy, empowerment, and education. We call for more resources to develop national strategies of advocacy and action to increase the witness of the United Church of Christ for a Just Peace. We call for the Office for Church in Society to facilitate the coordination of this work.

9. STUDY GUIDE

Session One

AFFIRMATION

Just Peace is grounded in God's activity in creation. Creation shows the desire of God to sustain and not destroy the world. The creation anticipates what is to come: the history-long relationship between God and humanity and the coming vision of shalom, which pulls history toward the fulfillment of God's reign.

PRAYER

O God who creates and who bids us to join in the work of creation and set aside our impulses to destroy, keep ever before us your vision of shalom, and build in us the will to move ourselves and our world toward this vision.

One fact that represents a break with the past is the massive technological revolution in weapons. The awesome power of nuclear weapons was unveiled when the United States used the atomic bomb in Hiroshima and Nagasaki in 1945. Some who participated in making the bomb and in deciding to use it came to the conclusion that such a weapon should never be used again after the horrors of those bombings became apparent. With the creation of the atomic bomb, the institution of war changed forever.

Polarization between rich and poor is not new. Oppression is not new. What is new is the global nature of this division wherein the poverty of the South is directly related to the wealth of the North. Over the past two hundred years, colonial structures have transferred wealth from poorer countries to richer countries. These structures are now solidly in place, creating not just a "developed" North but an "underdeveloped" South.

Questions

- Is it the will of God to create weapons of mass destruction?
- How did systems of global oppression and injustice come about?
- What is the relationship between these two questions?
- What is our responsibility today in light of these realities?
- Are we developing the power to end God's creation?

Session Two

AFFIRMATION

Just Peace is grounded in covenant relationship. God creates and calls us into covenant, God's gift of friendship. God agrees to abide with the people. "I will make a covenant of peace with them; it shall be an everlasting covenant with them; and I will bless them and multiply them, and will set my sanctuary in the midst of them forevermore [Ezek. 37:26]." When God's abiding presence is embraced, human well-being results, *shalom*, the Hebrew word that can be translated "Just Peace."

PRAYER

God who calls us into covenant, who loves us, supports us, is present to us, who suffers with us, we give thanks for this friendship that is all around us and pray that we may be faithful to this covenant and, by so doing, build shalom.

FROM *A JUST PEACE CHURCH* (P. 138)

1. We affirm the unity of the whole human community and oppose any use of nationalism to divide this covenant of friendship.
2. We reject all labeling of others as enemies and the creation of institutions that perpetuate enemy relations.
3. We affirm diversity among peoples and nations and the growth and change that can emerge from

151

the interchange of differing value systems,
ideologies, religions, and political and economic
systems.
4. We affirm nonviolent conflict as inevitable and
valuable, an expression of diversity that is
essential to healthy relationships among people
and nations.

QUESTIONS

- In what ways do you experience tension between your
faith and your patriotism?
- What could the United Church do to end the Cold
War? What could we do to achieve better relations
with poor countries?
- Do you think conflict is good or bad?

Session Three

AFFIRMATION

Just Peace is grounded in the reconciling activity of
Jesus Christ. Human sin is the rejection of the covenant
of friendship with God and one another and the creation
and perpetuation of structures of evil. Through God's
own suffering love on the cross, the power of these
structures has been broken and the possibility for
relationship restored. The coming of Christ is the seal of
our friendship with God, when God speaks peace to the
people.

PRAYER

Come, Christ Jesus. We have turned our back on you. We have turned our back on one another. We have structured our community so as to oppose one another and to do violence. Come, Christ Jesus. Let us hear your word of peace. Let our hostile communities experience the surprise of your suffering love. Come, Christ Jesus.

FROM *A JUST PEACE CHURCH* (PP. 141-43)

3. We affirm that war must be eliminated as an instrument of national policy and the global economy must be more just. To meet these goals, international institutions must be strengthened.

6. We reject any use of threat to use weapons and forces of mass destruction and any doctrine of deterrence based primarily on using such weapons. We also reject unilateral full-scale disarmament as a currently acceptable path out of the present international dilemma. We affirm the development of new policies of common security, using a combination of negotiated agreements, new international institutions and institutional power, nonviolent strategies, unilateral initiatives to lessen tensions, and new policies which will make the global economy more just.

7. We affirm the mutual and verifiable freeze on the testing, production, and deployment of nuclear weapons as the most important step in breaking the escalating dynamics of the arms race, and call upon the United States and the Soviet Union, and other nations to take unilateral initiatives toward implementing such a freeze, contingent upon the

other side responding, until such a time as a comprehensive freeze can be negotiated.

8. We declare our opposition to all weapons of mass destruction. All nations should:
   a. declare that they will never use such weapons;
   b. cease immediately the testing, production, and deployment of nuclear weapons;
   c. begin dismantling these arsenals;
   d. while the process of dismantling is going on, negotiate comprehensive treaties banning all such future weapons by any nation.

9. We declare our opposition to war, violence, and terrorism. All nations should:
   a. declare that they will never attack another nation;
   b. make unilateral initiatives toward dismantling their military arsenals, calling upon other nations to reciprocate;
   c. develop mechanisms for international law, international peacekeeping, and international conflict resolution.

QUESTIONS

• In what ways can war be eliminated? Does the church have a role?
• Is a call to all nations realistic? Why? Why not?
• How can you act effectively to eliminate war?

Session Four

AFFIRMATION

Just Peace is grounded in the presence of the Holy Spirit. We have not been left alone in history. God sends the Holy Spirit to continue the struggle to overcome the powers ranged against human bonding. Thus our hope for a Just Peace does not rest on human efforts alone, but on God's promise that we will "have life and have it abundantly [John 10:10]."

PRAYER

Spirit of the living God, let us feel your power. Spirit of the living God, let us recognize your presence moving even in the midst of those whom governments seek to repress. Spirit of the struggle for justice and peace, awaken our passion and our commitment. Amen.

FROM *A JUST PEACE CHURCH* (P. 139)

1. We affirm all nations working together to ensure that people everywhere will be able to meet their basic needs, including the right of every person to:
   a. food and clean water
   b. adequate health care
   c. decent housing
   d. meaningful employment
   e. basic education
   f. participation in community decision making and the political process

g. freedom of worship and religious expression
h. protection from torture
i. protection of rights without regard to race, sex, sexual orientation, religion, or national or social origin
2. We affirm the establishment of a more just international order in which:
    a. trade barriers, tariffs and debt burdens do not work against the interests of the poor and developing nations;
    b. poor nations have a greater share in the policies and management of global economic institutions.

QUESTIONS

• When you read in the newspapers of poor people protesting, do you ever think this might be the work of the Holy Spirit?
• Do all people have a right to their basic human needs? If so, how can that right be realized?
• Will we ever eliminate the institution of war if we ignore the presence of injustice? What is the relation of injustice and peace?

Session Five

AFFIRMATION

Just Peace is grounded in the community of reconciliation: the Just Peace *church.* Jesus, who is our peace (Ephesians 2:14), visibly and tangibly announced and enacted God's reign on earth.

Jesus performed signs of forgiveness and healing and made manifest that God's reign is for those who are in need. The church is a continuation of that servant manifestation. As a Just Peace church, we embody a Christ fully engaged in human events as the fulfilling of God's promise to befriend the people. The church is thus a real countervailing power to those forces that divide, that perpetuate human enmity and injustice, that destroy.

PRAYER

We give thanks, Christ Jesus, for your church. We give thanks that you, who befriended all people, have called us into your church to befriend the people. We are too much aware of the forces that would stop us. We pray for courage, courage to be your church.

FROM *A JUST PEACE CHURCH* (PP. 81-82)

The Just Peace church is a church that organizes itself and functions for God's radical mission of justice and peace to the world. Its being is proclaimed and lived by the "gospel of peace," which it shares with the world (Ephesians 6:15; Romans 10:15; Isaiah 52:7). Its life under the rule of Christ is marked by a continual searching for "the things that make for peace [Luke 19:42; Rom. 14:19]."

The Just Peace church proclaims God's promise of peace and justice for all and works to fulfill that promise. The Just Peace church, in proclaiming and doing, is continually growing in faith in Jesus Christ and understanding of the centrality of peacemaking to the gospel. It works unceasingly to expand the vision of a Just Peace and seeks to discover new and creative ways to build Just Peace. The Just Peace church equips its members for God's mission and exemplifies in its own life the peace that God gives to the world.

QUESTIONS

- Is your local church presently a Just Peace church? Why? Why not?
- What would it take to help your church start on the road to a Just Peace?
- What steps can your group take to begin that process?

Session Six

AFFIRMATION

Just Peace is grounded in *hope*. Shalom is the vision that pulls all creation toward a time when weapons are swept off the earth and all creatures lie down together without fear, where all have their own fig tree and dwell secure from want. As Christians, we offer this conviction to the world: peace is possible.

PRAYER

God who is in our past, nurturing us; God who is in our future, beckoning us; God who is all around us, empower us to live our lives and build our churches and communities so that they make visible our hope in you. Amen.

From *A Just Peace Church* (pp. 66-67)

To base a national policy on the fear of death is to lose the vision of the state as an order based on justice. The loss of this vision has resulted in public policy that is based on apocalypticism and despair.

The church can contribute to the public policy debate over peace and the nuclear threat in many ways, but here we raise up two.

First, the church must constantly provide a prophetic critique of the state when the state fails to implement policy aimed at the fulfillment of justice. The hope for human community confronts the economies of greed. The church regards this prophetic critique as a contribution to the public policy debate because the church is capable of offering an alternative view to the prevailing understanding of national security as the supreme justification of the use of any amount of force in the protection of the nation-state. On the contrary, the church offers a conception of the state as justifying its existence through the creation of justice.

Second, the church contributes a vision of human hope, without which alternatives to deterrence theory cannot emerge. The church must make clear in the public policy debate that prevailing theories of the human situation as solely one of violent aggrandizement are one-sided and distorted. Forgiveness is possible and trust can emerge. In raising human hope in the public policy debate over nuclear weapons, we in the church pose an important countervailing force in the political process.

- Do you believe peace is possible? Do you believe there will ever be a time when the institution of war will be eliminated?
- Has our nation adopted deterrence theory because it does not have enough hope? What are the *alternatives* to deterrence?
- Is the primary purpose of the state to achieve justice and well-being? How does this relate to national security and deterrence?
- As Christians, what unique role do we play in working for a world at peace?